The

The Ghost Hunter's Field Guide

The Ghost Hunter's Field Guide

The Ghost Hunter's Field Guide

By Margie Kay

Published by 7th Planet Productions
PO Box 1166
Independence, MO 64051

©Copyright 2010 By Margie Kay
All Rights Reserved.

No part of this book may be reprinted or reproduced by any means, electronic or mechanical, including recording, photocopying, or by information storage or any other form in whole or in part without express written permission of the author.

ISBN 978-0-557-38701-4

First Edition

Set in Bewilder and Garamond typefaces

All photographs, unless otherwise noted, are copyrighted
by Margie Kay, Dennis Kindle, Rich Carter, and HearthMasters, Inc.

Cover design by Maria Christine
Cover model: Rachel Cline
Contact: Margie Kay at margiekay06@yahoo.com
or write to the above address.

The Ghost Hunter's Field Guide

Acknowledgements

Dedicated to my mother, aunt, grandmothers,
grandfathers, and my spirit guide, White Cloud-
who all communicate with me from the other side,
and who encouraged me to write this book.

Special thanks to Maria Christine for her editing assistance
and to Patti Colbert for her assistance with research.

The Ghost Hunter's Field Guide

Table of Contents

Introduction.. 7

Chapter 1 What are Ghosts?... 11

Chapter 2 Contacting Spirits............................... 20

Chapter 3 Descriptions of Non-Physical Entities:
The Lecher, Time Imprint, Aliens, Poltergeist, Demons, Orbs, Fog and Apparitions, Plasma, Ball Lightning, Spirit Fog, Tree Sprites, Fairies, Shadow People, Handling Encounters with Negative Entities……...………………….. 30

Chapter 4 How to Communicate With Ghosts:
Margie's Meditation Method, Other Ways to Raise Your Level of Consciousness and Vibratory Rate, How to Communicate With Ghosts Using Your Sixth Sense……….. 49

Chapter 5 Ghost Hunting Tools and Techniques:
Laser Thermometer, Digital Thermometer, EMF Detector, Digital Cameras and Video, Motion-Activated Cameras, Night Vision, Digital Recorders, Wind Meter, Pendulums and Dowsing Rods, UV Light, Psychics, White Noise, How to Make Your Own Ghost Communicator, Wind or Fan, Drinking Glass, Other Devices, Your Ghost Hunting Kit…. 65

Chapter 6 How to Dowse for Spirits:
How to use dowsing equipment, How to make your own dowsing rod, How to make your own clay pendulum……… 73

Chapter 7 Photographing Ghosts:
How to Photograph Ghosts, Photos of anomalous objects……………………………………………………………... 81

Chapter 8 Good Places to Find Ghosts.................. 89

The Ghost Hunter's Field Guide

Table of Contents

Chapter 9 The Investigation Process
Interviewing Witnesses, Interview Form, Ruling out Other Possibilities, How to Get Rid of Ghosts........................... 92

Chapter 10 How to Protect Yourself While Ghost Hunting: White Light, Crystals, Encounters with Negative Entities... 110

Chapter 11 Real Ghost Hunts:
Ghost Hunt Experiences, Haunted Chimneys..................... 117

Chapter 12 66 Famous Haunted sites to Visit............... 195

Chapter 13 Paranormal Radio and TV Shows............... 220

Chapter 14 Resources... 224

Chapter 15 Glossary of Paranormal Terms.................. 228

Bibliography... 243

Index.. 247

The Ghost Hunter's Field Guide

Introduction

How I got involved in Ghost Hunting

I was raised in the Kansas City area by my father, who was a salesman for Encyclopedia Britannica- and my mother, who was a housewife for 17 years. Mom had a Bachelor's Degree in Business, but she felt it was more important to stay home with me and my younger sister and brother, and at that time most mothers didn't work anyway. Mom was largely responsible for seeing that I succeeded in school. Both of my parents were very intelligent, but my father has a genius level IQ, as did his father and two grandfathers. This may explain why he understood my growing abilities as a psychic, although he didn't discuss this with me during my childhood. He has since spent much time studying and becoming a proficient healer and psychic.

Neither of my parents ever told me to stop seeking answers, or had any fears about my abilities as many people do. This open attitude of both of my parents likely allowed me to accept more and more experiences.

I remember seeing energy fields around trees at the age of five, and by age eleven I could see and talk to ghosts, see future events, and communicate with my cat telepathically. At first all of this was a little frightening, but after a few years I got used to it, and realized that ghosts found me because I could see and talk to them while others did not. In school, however, I was very shy and kept to myself because I was afraid of what others might say if they found out what I could do. I lost some friends because they didn't understand me.

  I developed an interest in the paranormal and borrowed lots of books from the library to study. I was also curious about UFOs, although at the time I did not realize that I had actually had contact with UFOs. I wouldn't find out until years later under hypnosis that UFO contact began when I was 16 months old and continued throughout my life. I mention this because I feel that the UFO contact is responsible for much of my clairvoyant abilities because after each significant UFO encounter, my abilities noticeably increased.

  My mother bought me a book about Edgar Cayce when I was 15, which was my first exposure to others, had similar experiences to mine. Once in a while Dad bought me a UFO magazine to read. Although neither of my parents knew how to help me since they had no personal experience with clairvoyance, clairaudience, telepathy, and clairsentience, they didn't hesitate to get materials that I could use for research.

  At age 15, while I was a sophomore in high school, my science teacher introduced Extra Sensory Perception to the class. I was thrilled that he had an interest in the subject, but didn't mention my own experiences with ESP. The teacher tested everyone in the class using the famous *Rener* cards that include a square, circle, wavy lines, even cross, and a star. I scored so high that he insisted on doing more testing with me after class, and this turned into a three-month long experiment every afternoon after school with the teacher and two other students. They tested me with a 52-card deck, numbers, letters, and anything they could think of, and asked me to try to foretell future events and diagnose illness.

At the same time the testing was going on I started to see more ghosts in my house. I already knew there were spirits there because I could feel their presence, but this was different. There were many three-dimensional faces in the walls of the hallway and bathroom that moved and spoke, although I could not hear what they said. We also experienced footsteps, doors banging, and lights going off and on by themselves, with most of the activity happening when I was in the house... My cat, whiskers, would sometimes look at some invisible thing on the ceiling or wall, and then run out of the room.

I gradually became more sensitive to spirits, and one day watched a scene from the past unfold before me in my bedroom. A woman dressed in an 1880's style black dress and wide brimmed hat killed a younger woman with a large butcher knife. I could see the younger woman screaming, but again, heard no sound along with it. This was especially disturbing and I thought I might have lost my mind until my science teacher recommended that we research this large home.

I found that the house had been built in the 1850's and was a doctor's hospital in the later 1800's, and that there had been several mysterious deaths in the house during the time that the doctor owned it. And coincidentally, the mansion just two doors down had a dark history to it as well, so it is no wonder that the area was active with spirits.

By the time I reached 21 years of age I started doing psychic readings for people by answering any questions they had, looking into their future, and checking for medical issues they should be aware of. The readings helped to supplement my income from my job as a professional musician. By practicing on hundreds of people, I got better and better. However, I soon found out that when you are an open channel this can allow some dark entities to enter your life, and so had to learn how to protect myself from these forces.

At age 22 I got my first official missing person case with a private investigator, who was working on a case in Kansas. I was able to find the location of the kidnapper, find out why they did it, discover who else was involved, and see when the best time would be for them to go in to rescue the child. The next day I got a thankful call from the child's aunt, who told me that they couldn't believe how accurate my information was and that the child was found unharmed. If they hadn't arrived when they did, the girl would have been going into a white slavery ring the next day. After that I decided that I needed to work with law enforcement and private investigators, which I continue to this day. I no longer charge for finding missing persons, and am happy to help anyone who asks.

Ghost hunting is now a serious hobby for me and that is why I founded the non-profit association, *Quest Investigation Group*. *QUEST* is comprised of a team of investigators trained in forensics, investigation and intuitive investigation. The team does ghost hunting at the request of homeowners or building owners in an effort to gain scientific evidence of ghosts and other entities, and to improve communication with those who have traveled to the other side.

I have had good luck working with a team of people and I suggest the same for others working in this field. This book approaches the subject of ghost hunting in a slightly different manner that normal, using not only scientific tools to capture evidence, but also the use of the sixth sense in locating, communicating, and gaining information about spirits.

I hope you find this book interesting and useful in your own ghost hunting endeavors.

Margie Kay

CHAPTER 1

What are Ghosts?

> "I heard that kind of a sound that a ghost makes when it wants to tell about something that's on its mind and can't make itself understood, and so can't rest easy in its grave, and has to go about that way every night grieving."
>
> — Mark Twain

Just what are ghosts? I have some opinions based on my years of research on the subject and experience in contacting people who have passed on. Since I can usually readily communicate with the spirit of a deceased person, and they often answer questions that only that person's family would know, it is obvious that I am really speaking to the true spirit of that person. In case you are worried about a "false spirit" coming through, we have methods of protection against that sort of thing and always use them before any communication—see more on that topic later in the book.

In some rare cases where I can't speak to the spirit directly, I will get the "essence" of the person and know what their personality was and what their answer might be. This might sound very odd, but the only way I can explain it is that I know what they would say if they were here.

I have also had encounters with other entities besides ghosts—including aliens, orbs, rods, poltergeists, tiny white lights, fairies or angels, and strange, unexplainable creatures. I believe that these types of beings exist in a higher dimension and are able to come to our Third/Fourth dimension at certain times to do whatever it is they wish. It is clear that they are observing living humans much of the time. What is not so clear is exactly what they are and why they are observing us. All I know is that I sense that they are all here for a reason and that even though we may not yet have the capability of understanding them, nevertheless they do exist.

I see the vibratory rate or energy field of living beings. This field is in and around the body and aura and looks like layers of energy just above the skin or surface, then extends to about three feet out in all directions. It vibrates or shakes. <u>All living things and metals, rocks, etc. have an electromagnetic energy field, which is measurable. Most humans emit approximately 7 volts of electricity</u>,

<u>which can be detected with a voltmeter; therefore, we have an electromagnetic field as well.</u>

 Spirits probably have a much higher vibration than living people. I believe that each dimension has a range of vibration, and beings that are in tune with that dimension call that space their home and exist in it. For instance, we, in our physical bodies, may not be able to move to another dimension even if we wanted to. But take us out of that body: in the astral body if alive, or in spirit form if dead, and we can easily move through our third (physical) and fourth (time) dimensions we are familiar with, as well as the fifth dimension.

 Theoretical Physicist Dr. Michio Kaku states on his website mkaku.org that "…many physicists believe (but cannot yet prove) that the universe at the instant of the Big Bang was in fact fully ten dimensional." Kaku says that some physicists believe that light is actually from the fifth dimension, and that only part of it crosses over into our fourth dimensional world. Communications I've had with my mother and others, who have passed over to the other side, have been on the topic of spirits made of light photons, which reside in the fifth dimension, and sometimes cross into our world. If only scientists and mediums could get together to study this, perhaps someday we can have definitive proof about what happens to our spirit after death of the body.

 Take a look at the electromagnetic spectrum on the next page and you'll see what I'm talking about. There are measurable radio waves, cosmic waves, visible color spectrum, etc. that our scientists have determined have different lengths of waves or vibration. I suspect that just above the visible light spectrum is the next dimension up—the fifth—just a little further up the scale than normal perceptions will allow. Psychics may more easily see this level because they vibrate at a higher rate and are more "in tune" with that level.

As an example of how "tuning" works, if you put a stringed instrument in a place by itself, and then play another stringed Instrument of the same type in the same room, the first instrument will sound by itself. Try playing the A string on a violin and then listen to the other violin and you'll hear it sound. This is similar to a psychic tuning in to a vibration of similar rate or value.

Another explanation for apparitions may be what I call a *Time Imprint*. Other investigators have come to this conclusion as well. I base this on the fact that some "ghosts" look like they are going about their daily activities and are completely unaware of the observer.

There is no communication with the observer whatsoever and the observer cannot get a reaction from the "ghost." Most paranormal investigators believe that some buildings, perhaps because of the materials used in construction, record events that are played back later just like a movie. In fact, in some investigations for missing persons, I watch what looks like a movie of the scene and see exactly what happened. Most of the time it is not pleasant, and I don't enjoy doing it, but it is a way to determine the sequence of events.

So how is it that some of us see ghosts and some do not? I believe it has something to do with genetics and practice. Genetically, some of us may inherit genes from our ancestors that allow us to use our sixth sense (and seventh and so on) more readily than other people. Just as someone may be predisposed to be a great golfer, another might be naturally very psychic. Since my own family is now four generations of psychics, and I know many other psychic families as well, this is strong evidence to support the theory of genetics having something to do with the sixth sense.

The Ghost Hunter's Field Guide

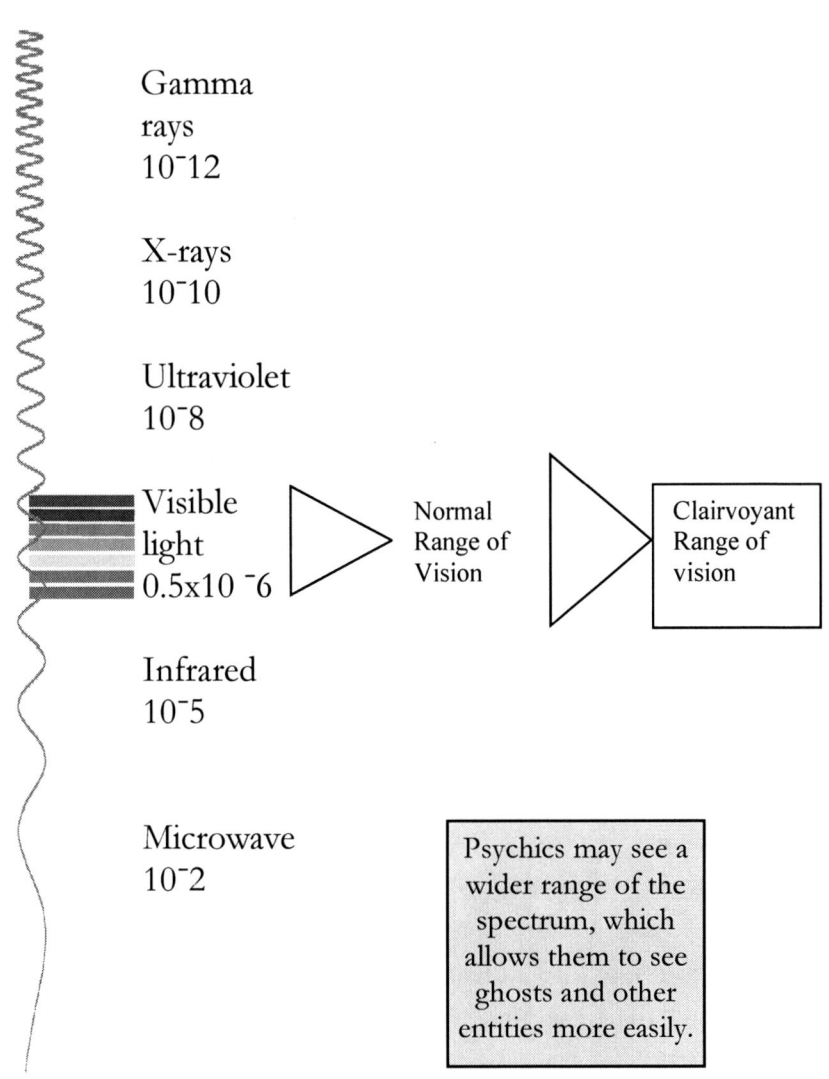

Gamma rays 10^{-12}

X-rays 10^{-10}

Ultraviolet 10^{-8}

Visible light 0.5×10^{-6} — Normal Range of Vision — Clairvoyant Range of vision

Infrared 10^{-5}

Microwave 10^{-2}

Psychics may see a wider range of the spectrum, which allows them to see ghosts and other entities more easily.

The Electromagnetic Spectrum

Practice also has a great deal to do with the ability to communicate with the other side. Children are more open about these subjects than an adult. The child has not yet been told that he can't see these things or that they are not really there, so he does not know that he shouldn't see them. If the child is allowed to grow up without prejudice about whether or not something such as a ghost does exist—he will learn to accept and communicate with the other side and may also remember past lives. This may also be the source of imaginary friends.

This knowledge can be a great benefit emotionally because we have confirmation that our ancestors really do look out for us, as is evidenced by the many people who are saved from harm by their loved ones who have passed on. You may feel better now knowing that you don't need to feel the sense of loss so badly when someone passes over, and that you will live on as well.

There have been numerous occasions where a spirit helped me or other members of our family. In August of 2006 my youngest daughter had an emergency C-section to save her baby. The baby was just under 32 weeks gestation. For some reason, she came to work 45 minutes early that day, and it was a good thing because we were able to rush her to the hospital immediately. The baby was less than four pounds and had to remain in a neonatal care unit for six weeks. During that time, he contracted a Staph infection from a catheter in his arm that was used to deliver food and medication directly to the blood.

The baby was thriving and doing well for about two weeks, and then he started to lose weight. This was not a good sign, and the doctors and nurses could not figure it out. One day, a nurse suddenly got the idea to do a test for Staph, even though she thought it would be remote possibility. The result was positive.

Fast treatment with antibiotics worked and the baby got well quickly. If it had gone on further without treatment he might not have survived.

My mother died the month before this occurred, and I was surprisingly in communication with her right away. She told me that she mentioned the Staph test to the nurse so she would act on it. We believed it.

Other examples of this have occurred as warnings of future events. One day I heard the voice of my grandfather while I was driving in my car. He said "Take another street" and I immediately turned to take another route. I later found out there was a big accident on the street I normally travel on.

Another communication from the other side occurred when I was 17 years old. My mother was driving with me in the front seat and my 13-year-old brother was in the back seat. A sudden ice storm came up as we drove North on 71 Highway from Springfield to Kansas City, and produced black ice on the road. I suddenly saw golden light around me and heard my grandfather's voice say "put on your seat belts." My grandfather had been dead for several years.

This was during a time when no one wore seat belts. I told my mother and brother to buckle up as I hooked up my seatbelt. Not five minutes later, my mother lost control of the car on the ice and we spun around, and then headed towards a big drop-off head-on into a guard rail. We were going so fast that I thought surely we would go over the railing, but didn't. We all came out of the accident with minor injuries, except for my mother's broken nose. If we hadn't had our seatbelts on we surely would have been badly injured.

In 1976 my sister, Alice, went on a trip to Colorado with her best friend and her family over the July 4th week. She was 16 at the time. The group was getting ready to go out and Alice was fixing her hair when an apparition of my deceased grandfather suddenly appeared in the mirror. Alice turned around, but the vision disappeared. She knew something was wrong and called home, but couldn't get anyone to answer the phone. She was panicked. Later that night I was awakened at four O'clock in the morning by my grandfather's voice saying "contact your mother." I also knew something was wrong.

At that time I was living in Carrollton, Missouri in a tiny apartment with my new husband and no phone, so called the next day and could not get an answer. It was a few days before we found out that there had been a house fire on July 4th caused by kids shooting bottle rockets at the wood shingled roof. My mother, grandmother, and brother had all been moved to a temporary apartment, and were all ok.

Over the years I've honed my skills to the point that I can now speak with almost anyone who has passed over, as long as I have their name and place that they once lived. The vibration of the name is what I tune into. This is easier to do if there is some important reason to get in touch with someone who has passed over- apparently, the more emotion around a passing the better for contact. In the case of solving a murder, there is a lot of emotion involved so contact is fairly easy.

I am in almost constant contact now with both my grandfathers, grandmothers, my mother, and a spirit named White Cloud, who was a Native American in this area. White Cloud says I was a member of his tribe in a former life many centuries ago and was a healer and shaman named "Medicine Woman." All of my guides give me advice and assistance on different issues and help with cases I work on.

My grandfather Lombardo told me that he sits on a council of 13 members who are guardians for a large group of people. He is the guardian of our family as well, which makes sense because that is what he did in life. We are a large Italian (on my mother's side) family and all who remember him say my grandfather was the token "Godfather" of the family and made sure everyone was taken care of. Whenever there is something that could cause potential harm to a family member, even to his great grandchildren that he never met, grandfather Lombardo gives us a warning by appearing to us.

The contact I have with all of my guides is similar to speaking one-on-one with a person as if they were physically in the room with me, but we communicate telepathically. I hear their voices clearly and just to test myself at times—I have someone else ask something I could not possibly know about and my guides give me the answer.

Sometimes I'll ask for some piece of information that only the person I'm working with and the spirit could know about, and they never fail to either show or tell me something unique. This is usually the way I'll start a communication in order to make sure that I'm talking to the right person. The spirit will give me details such as their favorite eye shadow color, or what is in the wallet that now belongs to their son.

Talking with ghosts is how I got interested in haunted sites and ghost hunting. As a researcher, I am looking for proof of the existence of spirits, which is proof that we all live on even after death of the body.

CHAPTER 2

Contacting Spirits

"I figure I basically am a ghost. I think we all are."

John Astin

During trance state, I contact spirits and have conversations with them, just like I would with a living person. I have learned how to put myself in a light trance state without the assistance of a hypnotist, and this is very helpful when contacting those who have passed over. The answers are offered telepathically, which I hear as regular voices. The spirits tell me they are not "dead," but that they are most assuredly alive and in fact, are more alive in spirit than when they are in a human body. They say that they felt trapped while in a human body, but when in spirit form feel very free.

I'd like to share a conversation with you that I had with my mother shortly after her death, which explains a lot about the spirit world.

Contact with Marie Lombardo
July 19, 2006
11:30 pm

I was meditating while sitting on our porch one evening when Mom popped into my head. Since my brother Frank and I had told her we would try to contact her on the 11th of every month, I shouldn't have been surprised to see her appear, but since it was only a week after her death I wasn't expecting to be able to talk to her so soon. After all, it took 30 years for my grandfather to contact me after his death, so I thought it would be awhile for her a well. Mom asked if I wanted to know anything, and I said, yes, there were some things I'd like to know about the afterlife that I'd like to hear from her directly. I asked what kind of a body the spirit was made of and how it traveled around. She told me some very remarkable things:

> "The spirit body is made of light photons. It is a very subtle body, yet it does have measurable mass. This body usually travels as a ball of light—you have seen them as orbs– because it is easier that way. Then when the spirit arrives at its destination it can form into whatever shape it desires, in the case of someone who recently passed he/she would appear to the person as that old body so he will be recognized. But the spirit body can form into whatever it wants, and in fact, can be in multiple locations at the same time. It can even choose to incarnate in the body of an animal or plant, or even other beings on other planets if it desires."

Wow. Can you, say, visit with two people at once?

> "The choice to live in a particular living physical body is up to the spirit – the choice having to do with what the spirit needs to experience in order to grow, or even just to have an experience to know about it. It doesn't always have to do with growth of the soul. The spirit can split up into many parts and have several lifetime experiences all at once. This is why some people have dreams or visions of other locations and families that they feel are familiar to them—or Déjà vu. Part of the soul had that experience and brought it home to the rest of itself. You may have seen balls of light at some time and then saw that appeared to split into several smaller orbs. This is the same soul—just different parts of it."

"There is also something you should know about death. The soul is more at home in its spirit body without the encumbrance of a physical body, and so in a manner of speaking "death" might mean just the opposite to a spirit. In other words, it is somewhat of a death to be in a living, physical body that is very restrictive. The soul body can move about at will, has no health problems, does not need to eat as you know it (we get fuel from the essence of plants), and can pretty much do what it wants. In fact, I can visit all of my relatives that passed over before me, all of my living relatives, and whoever else I want to visit at any time. I can also travel anywhere on the planet and to any other planet. Somewhat like Astral Travel. The astral body moves around in a similar fashion to the soul body and this is another method of communicating with those on this side. You have done this but don't use it as often as trance work. It is different in that the astral body not only sees everything around it like you do in trance, but it is clearer and you can physically touch and feel things, too."

Can you, say, visit with two people at once?

"Yes, absolutely. And in different times."

In different *times?*

"Well, time as you know it. There is no time where I am. But I can appear to you at my age of 10 or 75 if I wish—whatever might be appropriate. You have experienced this yourself when talking to mother and dad (she means her mother and father) and have seen them at different ages."

This conversation was quite incredible and really helped me understand "death" better. I am no longer as afraid to cross over and when the time comes I am sure it will be very pleasant. I hope that this will help people have a greater understanding of death of the body. Since that conversation I have seen my mother appear at many different ages. She says she and her family often go back to visit their house where they lived while she was growing up and they all go back to the ages they were at the time. I wonder if the current homeowners see them.

Trance Session, August 2006

During this trance session I asked to see the source of our family heritage and psychic abilities. Two beings, one male and one female, appeared to me. They walked on a hill in Ireland that was covered with old trees. They both had very long white hair, and long robes, yet looked middle-aged. I could sense however, that they were both very, very old and very intelligent. I believe that this perhaps genetic connection is the reason why I have a close connection to trees and tree spirits.

The male spirit spoke, and told me that my family DNA has some of their genetic material from many thousands of years ago. These tree spirits once walked the earth in a human-like form and lived among humans for a long time, before leaving and going back into the trees. The humans had changed their relationship with nature and no longer had the awareness they once did, so the tree spirits had to step back. They seemed genuinely happy that I contacted them, and said that few humans did this anymore. I asked who they were and was told "Fir Non Goln." I then said this out loud, and channeled several other sentences the spirits spoke, which was an unknown language to me and the other members of my team that were assisting. We investigated this and found that the language is ancient Gaelic, something I had no knowledge of.

What it's like on the Other Side

During my trance sessions I've gathered a lot of information from my ancestors and guides about what it is like in the spirit world. Some of what they've told me is pretty amazing and they've been insistent that I write this information down and share it with as many people as possible. Following is a list of things my guides would like everyone to know:

- When the body dies you will feel light, happy and free with no pain or discomfort. If you had a painful illness or injury in life you'll be very relieved not to be in that body any more. There is always someone waiting for you in spirit when you leave your body. That person is most likely someone you knew in life – like a trusted family member. They may be accompanied by other family members and there may be a spirit guide there you'll recognize as your guardian. These entities will tell you what to expect and help you through the transition. You'll be taken through the lifetime you just left from birth to death doing a life review. You'll be able to see all of the good and bad things you did to help the progress of your soul. Then you'll get to watch your funeral and spend time with family members. Some family and friends may be aware of your presence.

- Soon you will learn how to travel around. You are a tiny ball of light photons with electrical energy now. You can move from place to place very quickly in this form. You may change your form to something more familiar if you wish, but this is not necessary. If you are able to communicate with the living, you may learn how to take energy from batteries or other energy sources in order to form a recognizable shape, but this method usually takes some time to perfect. Spirits readily communicate with each other and with trance mediums. Spirits may witness astral travelers or aliens passing by as well. Aliens don't inhabit this plane, but they pass through it to get to and from Earth.

- Ghosts/Spirits retain their personality when they pass over. This is why there are both "good" and "bad" ghosts – if they were bad in life, they'll usually still be bad in death and vice-versa. There is no automatic awakening or rising of consciousness at the moment of death, and I've been told that there is no heaven or hell as usually described by some religions. This is something your guides will explain. There are however, multiple dimensions, and as the consciousness is raised the spirit will be able to inhabit those realms. The spirit works with guides through many lifetimes and periods in-between lifetimes in spirit to work on raising its vibrations in order to experience the higher realms.

- Your soul is the part of you that is always alive and can never die. The earthly body is just a temporary body for the spirit to inhabit, and that is the only part that dies at death. The spirit recognizes this and remembers it at the time of death. The concept of reincarnation used to be taught in all of the world's religions but has been removed from some religious teachings in order to instill fear and make people behave a certain way.

- You may decide to stay in spirit or to reincarnate on the earth or somewhere else in the Universe. Most people from Earth reincarnate on Earth because it is familiar. They also reincarnate as humans in the same family groups since they feel comfortable with those other spirits. Often family members will have experiences as each other's children, siblings, spouses, parents, and grandparents. However, if a person wanted he/she could reincarnate as an animal or even a plant or rock, depending on the type of experience needed or desired. This usually does not happen until the person has raised his vibratory rate to a certain level.

- Spirits can incarnate on other planets as well as our own. If coming here directly from another planet, a person may feel like he doesn't belong here and feel out of place and like he doesn't "fit in." It makes take several generations for this feeling to go away. A lot of recently incarnated spirits often look at the stars a night and have a sense of "not belonging."

Many people wonder why spirits don't give us the lottery numbers or give us exact dates of future events, or warn us about catastrophes. The fact is that no one has the answers to those questions. Occasionally, you'll hear about someone winning the Powerball who says they got the numbers from their deceased grandfather in a dream. And my own grandfather seems to specialize in showing me pictures of future world events, and has been correct about the next volcano, earthquakes, and tsunami's many times. However, getting an exact date about an event seems to be the most difficult, probably since the spirit world, or fifth dimension, does not experience time as we know it.

When researching past events, however, the spirits seem to be very willing and helpful, often giving precise information like dates, names, and addresses. That makes communication with ghosts through telepathy a useful tool to use when ghost hunting.

Some people who have had UFO sightings or close encounters also have a "haunted" house. During my investigation of strange case involving Richard and Lori Carter in Butler, Missouri, we have determined that the connection between aliens and ghosts is probable. The Carters have obtained multiple photos of not only aliens and craft, but also have seen ghostly apparitions and misty forms taking shape in the same area. Some of these encounters have been in or near graveyards and others near farms. They often have paranormal experiences such as loud banging in the house after going out in the evening to get photographic evidence.

In an effort to get some answers about this strange connection I asked my mother about it one day, and she not only answered but showed me a scene from the Fifth dimension. In this scene I could see my deceased family members standing in an area along with other ghosts. They seemed to be in groups, floating along in the air above the Earth. Also in the scene were craft and alien beings moving or floating through the area not far from the spirits and live persons travelling in astral bodies.

While I watched this, my mother told me that she and other spirits inhabit the fifth dimension, and that the aliens are from higher dimensions. The aliens ~~and~~ must move through the fifth dimension to get to the third/fourth dimension (Earth). The spirits and aliens did not interact with each other at the time I was watching. My mother told me that she does not communicate with them, but that my grandfather does.

See my upcoming book *The UFO Hunter's Field Guide* for more information about aliens.

The world of ghost hunting is what some call 'paranormal,' and that, in my opinion, is because we just don't fully understand what 'normal' is yet. That is to say, the spirit world is most likely a natural, normal event and place, and that just because science doesn't fully understand it yet, is not proof that it doesn't exist.

Those of us who hunt ghosts do so mostly because we are looking for enough evidence to convince ourselves and the skeptics that there is life after death of the body. If you are new to ghost hunting, please try some of the scientific and intuitive techniques listed in this book and I can almost guarantee success in contacting spirits from the other side.

CHAPTER 3

Descriptions of Non-Physical Entities

"I have never yet heard of a murderer who was not afraid of a ghost"

John Philpot Curran

People often want to know what the different types of entities are that we encounter during investigations. I'm listing some of the more common beings here for your reference.

The Lecher

Among the non-physical entities are some who mean us no harm, but that get their life force by taking energy from humans. They may attach themselves to a person, which can cause extreme fatigue for the host. I had one of these attached to me in 1985, and it was removed by another psychic who asked the entity to move on to something else like a cow or sheep, which happened to be nearby. She saw the entity as a black shadowy shape attached to my right side. After the entity was gone, I felt immediately better and no longer was so fatigued. When this type of entity is removed the person usually feels much better because their energy is no longer being drained. These types of beings seldom return.

Time Imprint

A time imprint is simply a recorded "movie" of events that plays over and over again. There is no spirit present; you are just seeing the movie play. Most ghost hunters suspect that the materials used in buildings such as plaster, nails, and paint somehow record events in a similar fashion to the way film does. The way to tell if this is indeed what you are seeing is if the "ghost" does not appear to see you or interact with you or anyone else in the room while you are there. Another indication is if the same exact scene plays itself over and over again. Time Imprints can be useful when trying to solve unanswered questions about events. Time Imprints are typically associated with someone doing the same routine over and over again in the same location, such as one case where every time a woman brushed her teeth before retiring she saw the reflection of a man walk behind her from the doorway towards the shower.

Poltergeists

A Poltergeist may or may not be an entity of a person who lived on the earth. Activity such as moving objects, pushing, objects thrown across the room, objects missing and sometimes found in other locations, banging in or on the walls, furniture being rearranged, etc. has been attributed to a person in the house who is going through an emotional time. It is most common when teenagers, especially girls, are living in the home. Teens are usually not aware that they are causing this activity, and it will normally pass after the child gets older. If the teenager phenomenon has been ruled out, then it is time to look at other possible sources.

Remember the movie "*Poltergeist*"? This is a true (but embellished for the movies) story about a family who experienced extremely violent phenomenon in their home, and found out later that they were living on a Native American burial ground. The ground was likely protected by spirits assigned to the area by the Native Americans long ago. It is best to thoroughly check out a location first before buying a
house to avoid trouble like this!

I did a poltergeist investigation in Kansas City in 1993 along with several other experienced mediums. We were requested to do a clearing for a woman who had nightly activity in her house. The spirit moved and broke dishes, glasses and other objects, threw things across the room, slammed doors, and stomped around the house. He appeared as a black shadowy human figure and walked through doors and walls. The homeowner reported hearing audible moaning sounds as well. This was getting out of hand and the owner needed help.

Upon arrival at the house, I found three psychics in the living room who were scared stiff and refused to assist us. They sensed a very powerful, negative spirit and were unable to confront it. Another medium and I scanned the entire house, and both of us were drawn to the front bedroom as the main location of the spirit. I went into a trance and saw a well underneath the bedroom that went many feet down. I saw the body of a man in the well. The man had been murdered. He wanted resolution and felt wronged, and was very angry about it.

The spirit of the man gained power from the people living in the house due to their fear of him, and also from a Native American spirit protector of the area. Perhaps the well I saw was a natural well cut into the stone many thousands of years ago.

The murder happened in the mid 1800's so the killer was long dead. After I explained this to the man he calmed down and a few minutes later the six of us (five mediums and the homeowner) saw a white ball of light about three feet in diameter move from the bedroom, through the living room and through three of us, and then out the far wall. We felt this entity move through us and all of us got cold chills. The homeowner reported back to us that she had no more activity in the house after that. In my experience, there may be other non-human entities that cause poltergeist activity, but they are rare.

Fairies

With the long history of fairies, 'faeries,' 'little people, or 'wee folk', especially in Ireland, England, Wales, and Scotland, don't rule out the possibility of their existence. The word 'fairy" is derived from the earlier term 'fay,' which in turn came from the Latin 'fata,' which means 'the fates.'

The ancient legends of elves, gnomes, leprechauns, and good and bad fairies from may well have some substance to them. The origin of these legends dates back to the ancient Irish 'Tuatha De Dannan' or "The Star People," (a connection to Extra-terrestrials perhaps?) and archaic Irish gods. The pre-Christian religious tradition in Ireland was known as the oral Faery Tradition or Feary-Faith.

The many stories that abound about fairies include encounters that involve hours, days, or even years of missing time, the disappearance of people altogether, help around the house, tricks or pranks on people, and much more. According to the Fairy-Faith.org many modern day encounters with fairies from all over the world have been reported. It is thought by some that people with Irish ancestry are more likely to have communication with fairies and there is an extra-terrestrial connection among the Irish as well.

My daughter and I have both seen what we believe to be fairies as well as an inter-dimensional gateway of some sort associated with the location where we saw them. My daughter actually disappeared for 45 minutes one day when she was just 5 years old while she ran through the area where the portal is located. If you see white, gold, or bluish-white orbs with feathered wings, or small beings that can't otherwise be explained, they may be fairies.

In my own experience and in other cases I've researched, it is a possibility that aliens may be disguising themselves as small fairies or gnomes (also known as a "screen memory") in order not to frighten the experience. When my youngest daughter was regressed in order to find out what happened to her with regards to alien encounters, we found out that her memory of gnomes in her room was incorrect and that they were actually small alien beings.

It is also possible that the fae are a different race of beings altogether.

Demons

There are exorcists and demonologists who specialize in dealing with demons. I don't. On one occasion, I saw three small creepy looking creatures that might be described as demons, but in fact, I don't know for sure what they were. They could easily have taken on a devilish appearance for effect or to scare me. I was 16 at the time and it was during my first astral travel experience, so I may have had some fears about evil entities before learning protection techniques. Since then, I've run into evil spirits, but so far, no demons. Real possessions are extremely rare, and other reasons for suspected possession should be thoroughly check out before calling in an expert.

Some UFO and ghost investigators believe that there is a correlation between the reptilian beings and demons and those they may be one and the same thing. There is much evidence that this is the case. The Reptilian creatures behave and look (scaly skin, vertical pupils, long fingers with claws) as we would expect a demon to—and may indeed be the source of the early Christian ideas about the devil and his minions

During trance sessions I have experienced the presence of reptilian-looking creatures that had a negative energy, but did not do any harm to anyone present while we were at the scene of the investigation. At a meeting with a friend one evening, I was surprised to see a very tall reptilian walk out of her body and stand to the side for a minute, then return. This certainly would be a form of possession; but my friend does not currently have any symptoms of anything out of the ordinary except for medical issues. They may be related to the reptilian possessor wonder how many humans are unknowingly harboring these unwanted parasites.

The UFO community has done extensive research on reptilians, so that is the place to look for more information. One book that may be especially helpful is David Icke's book *The Biggest Secret*, available at www.davidickebooks.co.uk for more information on this topic.

Some people are afraid to contact loved ones because they think the spirit could be a demon masquerading itself. However, if you protect yourself before contacting a spirit and ask to speak only to the person you request, no bad entity can come through. (See how to protect yourself later in this book) I believe that what you experience has to a large extent to do with what you believe. If you believe there are demons out there waiting to get you, they will. If you don't believe that, they probably won't bother you. I do caution you against ghost hunting if any doubts or fears along these lines or you could have a negative experience.

If you feel that a site is truly evil or that there is a demonic possession of the house or people living in it, get help from an expert demonologist like John Zaffis– www.johnZaffis.com, or NEAR-www.nearparanormal.com.

Orbs

Orbs, also known as balls, lights, or globes, are fairly common and many people see them with the naked eye or in photos. Orbs often show up in photographs but can often be attributed to reflections off of dust, moisture on lenses, or an out-of-focus lens. The orbs worth mentioning are the ones that appear to the naked eye and/or and float through space, go through walls or objects, appear to move under intelligent control, and look three-dimensional. If an orb has a face or other shape in it that is also worth noting. Some are very large and some are tiny.

I've done scans on several orbs in person and in photographs, and have come up with some possibilities as to what they are. In some instances the orb is a spirit. My deceased mother told me that spirits are made up of *light photons*; therefore, wouldn't it stand to reason that the spirit travels as a ball of light? It seems that they do travel from place to place, and time to time for that matter, in this manner then upon arrival may change into a more familiar body so people will recognize them.

Some orbs seem to be spirits that have never lived in a human body. They move about at will, and often appear to be investigating a location before moving on. In some instances orbs have been associated with fairies, sprites, angels, UFO sightings and crop circles, and have been seen moving into a UFO. They may be spirits of aliens, or perhaps are a probe of some sort. In any case, it's always exciting to get orbs on film. If you can take video of them you can sometimes tell if it looks like intelligence is in control as they move about.

Fog and Apparitions

Fog is less common than the appearance of orbs, but does appear on film and/or to the naked eye. It is often a non-distinct shape, forming and then disappearing, but sometimes forms a human or animal shape that may be very distinct and visible to the naked eye. The most common apparition is formed of a white, almost glowing misty substance. A full apparition, is the appearance of the entire body of a person and a partial apparition, is only part of the person. Some common partial apparitions appear as only the head, or the body without feet.

Some ghost researchers, me included, think that this is a form that a spirit can take on if they have obtained enough energy to do so. As an example, during a ghost hunt with 11 people, all of the batteries in the camcorders drained at the exact same moment, leaving the batteries in the still cameras alone. A second after that happened, we all saw a foggy apparition appear, although, not fully materialized. My theory is that the ghost needed electrical energy from the batteries in order to form a semi-physical form.

Plasma

Plasma is a visible light that appears during lightning storms, can be created by scientists in the lab, and has been seen during crop circle formation and poltergeist activity. It is extremely impressive to watch. Plasma is the fourth state of matter. Plasma is an ionized gas into which sufficient energy is provided to free electrons from atoms or molecules and to allow both ions and electrons, to coexist. It has appeared as very beams or balls of light.

Ball Lightning

I had the opportunity to see ball lighting (or plasma) when I was 10 years of age. There was a lightning storm going on and my father and mother yelled for me to come into the kitchen around 10:00 pm. I was astonished to see a brilliant white ball of light hovering above the open door of the cooking stove. It stayed for a minute, and then disappeared. My father told me it was rare ball lightening that had come down the stove vent, however, I found out later that ball lighting does not appear for more than a couple of seconds. So I am inclined to believe it was something else—maybe plasma or an unknown substance or entity.

Crop circle researcher Nancy Talbott, the Field Research Coordinator for the *BLT Research Team*, told me that she witnessed a beam of plasma coming from an unknown source outside her window during a visit to The Netherlands. The next morning, there was a gigantic crop circle in the neighboring field. The plasma appeared, as if on cue, right after she expressed the desire to a colleague to see a crop circle being formed. Ms. Talbott surmises that some form of consciousness heard her thoughts and created the circle for her to see. She has photos of this on her website at www.bltresearch.com.

Spirit Fog or Vortex

My friend Dennis Kindle gave me a photograph which shows a thick line of white fog that appeared during a spiritual ceremony in the woods in Arkansas right after a three-day crystal dig nearby. The men at the ceremony did not see this at the time, but it showed up on the photo, which was taken by someone outside the circle. The ceremony involved creating communication to the spirit world.

What is compelling is that this same zigzag shape is found painted on ancient spiritual sites and caves with petroglyphs, and is believed to be a symbol of communication with spirits.

There was definitely communication going on at the time the picture was taken. It would be interesting to get some pictures during other spiritual ceremonies to see what if more pictures can be taken of spirit fog.

Tree Sprites and Tree Spirits

I have been observing tiny white lights interacting with trees at many locations, but especially in my own backyard. I can only see the lights if I relax my eyes and "See," which is another term for using psychic vision with your eyes. The lights are only visible at night - probably because they would be difficult to see in sunlight. I began concentrating on looking at the lights around one particular tree, and one evening in 2005 I received a telepathic communication to ask the lights what they were. I thought that was strange, but did it nonetheless. To my astonishment, a male voice I've never heard spoke to me telepathically in a clear, loud voice, and said that the lights are the spirits of the tree or "Tree Sprites."

The sprites informed me that their purpose is to help the tree grow; tell it when to leaf and bud out, when to grow new limbs, and when to go dormant for the winter. One winter I noticed that that the sprites were unusually active, and watched as they made new limbs out of energy, which looked like dark three limbs with a white glow around them.

In the Spring I watched carefully to see if new limbs appeared where this energy had been created and sure enough, there were several!

I found out through our "talks" that these spirits have never been in human form, and that their purpose is to assist trees. They stay with the same tree for life, but when the tree dies the sprites will go to another nearby seedling. I've seen these white lights around trees since   Coincidentally, I recently purchased a book called *Irish Tree Spirits*, and after reading through it found out that a description I heard during the trance —'Fir Non Goln'—means "Spirits of the Trees."

The tree spirits also let me know that there is a Matrix of energy connecting one tree to the other, so they are connected to every tree on the planet. You can see this energy matrix coming off of each tree, reaching out to nearby trees. This energy looks like a dark line with a white field around it. It is possible to telepathically communicate with a tree, who in turn can request information from fellow trees in other locations and in other times, either in the past, present, or future. This is one way to connect with the Akashic record and get information about anything, including why ghosts haunt a certain location or what happened in the past that would cause a haunting. So trees can be a third-party communicator between an investigator and ghosts.

Aliens

There is quite possibly more evidence that aliens exist than there is evidence about ghosts! Since I have some experience investigating both, there are some similarities among them that you should be aware of.

While out ghost hunting you may run into other entities. There seems to be a correlation between alien and UFO sightings and paranormal activity in many cases. For instance, several research projects I'm working on that involve abductees or contactees, also involve what seems to be paranormal activity like unexplained sounds, voices, and objects moving, banging noises, missing objects, and orb, fog, and ghost sightings.

Aliens, like ghosts, seem to have the ability to walk through solid walls, appear and disappear at will, and fade in and out. They may be miss-identified as ghosts at times. We don't know yet what the connection is or why so many UFO-related cases also involve paranormal activity, however, there seems to be a pattern that can't be ignored, which is that intuitive or people with psychic abilities seem to experienced both alien and "paranormal' events. Some researchers put all of the above into the "Paranormal" category.

If you want more information about UFOs I suggest reading *Flying Saucers and Science* by nuclear physicist Stanton Friedman, MSc., or *Science Was Wrong* by Stanton Friedman and Kathleen Marden.

Shadow People

Shadow people do not appear to be "people" at all. They are usually described as being very dark, usually darker than a darkened room or "darker than night". They are typically six to six and one-half feet tall, without defined features and with or without red glowing eyes. The shadow people with red eyes seem to be more aggressive and want to cause fear. Some have been seen with no clothes, and others have mitten-link "hands." Some shadow people wear a wide-brimmed hat and long frock coat or cloak. The entire entity is black, even the face and hands, and the silhouette is usually of a man. Some have referred to these beings as "The Hat People."

Most encounters are fleeting, such as seeing a shadow out of the corner of the eye, but some reported experiences with shadow people are more frightening. Many sightings of shadow people are by persons sleeping, who suddenly wake up to see a dark figure standing near them and staring at them. Shadow people seem to be intensely interested in humans, as if they are observing us for some reason. I've encountered shadow people around graveyards, who seem to be observing spirits in the same manner as humans. There is no evidence to suggest that shadow people are spirits or are related to humans in any manner.

Some people have awakened in the middle of the night to a crushing feeling on their chest, and see a shadow person kneeling on them, and leaning over them face-to-face in an extremely menacing manner. Many say that they feel that the entity is stealing energy from them, or in some cases they believe that the being is attempting to take their soul or even their life. These encounters are thankfully, rare.

My family has had several encounters with shadow people. My oldest daughter saw a dark black entity, blacker than the night, standing in her bedroom when she was 13 years old. It stood there for at least 30 minutes, not moving, just staring at her. She felt a cold chill in the room and a negative energy, and was very frightened.

My own encounter occurred while driving home one evening after work at dusk. I saw a man standing on the steps of a church.

He was black from head to toe, and was wearing a long old fashioned 1800's style frock coat and a wide-brimmed hat. He stood there, staring at a building across the street with a scowl on his face. I got an eerie feeling and sense of anger from this being. As I drove by I saw him glance at me. A woman was exiting the building behind him, and then walked down the steps to the side of this shadow person, but she did not acknowledge him. I assume that she did not see him, because if she had there surely would have been a reaction. I was too shocked to stop the car, and kept driving. After I passed by I looked in the mirror and he was gone.

My 14-year old granddaughter awoke one night at 3:00 a.m. to see a shadow man with "mitten" hands standing in her room and watching the TV that she had turned off before she went to bed. Only static was on the TV. He was in front and to the side of her, but when she opened her eyes he almost immediately turned around to look at her, and then disappeared. She told me that she did not move or make a sound, but that the entity somehow knew she saw him. Since then, she and her family have had numerous sightings of shadow-like shapes and shadow people in their house.

Shadow people can also appear as dark, one-dimensional outlines on walls, which move about. Some move about very quickly, as if on a mission, others stop and seem to stare at humans before moving on. Some have been captured on film, but were not noticed at the time the photo was taken.

Sightings of shadow people are sometimes the cause of fear and nightmares in children and adults. Perhaps they are the real boogie man in the closet or under the bed. Most paranormal researchers, me included, do not believe that shadow people are ghosts or disembodied spirits, but are another type of as yet unknown entity. Many paranormal researchers believe that shadow people are from another dimension, and are here to observe humans, then return from where they came. The evidence suggests that these beings are a very powerful negative energy that should not be provoked.

I strongly suggest setting up protection around your house if you are seeing unexplained shadows (see how to protect yourself later in this book).

See descriptions of other less-common entities in the Glossary section of this book.

Your job as an investigator is to attempt to determine what or who is doing the haunting, so while ghost hunting keep in mind that everything that happens, and everything you see or hear may not be related to a deceased person, and it may be another form of life that we don't fully understand yet.

The Ghost Hunter's Field Guide

Handling Encounters with Negative Entities

There are negative spirits, just as there are negative people. I believe that the best practice is to leave them alone unless you have strong psychic abilities, a strong will, and proper training to confront these beings such as an expert like John Zaffis, nephew of the famous Ed and Lorraine Warren. Negative spirits and entities feed off of fear. They get their power from the power you give them unknowingly. If you can't face a negative entity without having fear about it—the best advice I can give you is don't do it.

I have faced several negative beings but the second experience I had was the most impressive. I'll share it with you so you can see how I handled it. I was 24 years old at the time and had been studying what most people would consider to be metaphysical subjects for several years. My father taught me several techniques for when I ran into something evil—which he assured me I would experience at some point in my life due to the fact that I am psychic. People who have their third eye open are subject to attack if they are not fully protected.

I played in a local rock band for over a year, and then left after the leaders, a man and wife, asked me to participate in a bizarre act. I really had no idea up to that point that these two were anything but average normal people, but it turned out that wasn't the case. In fact, they told me that they had the lead singer involved, too. I finally realized that I had been lured into a situation by persons more experienced in the esoteric and who followed a different, more sinister path. With my eyes wide open now, I could see these people for what they were—a couple of witches who practiced black magic. They didn't want me to leave for two reasons—and one was because they were losing their bass player. The other was because I wouldn't let them take my energy. Both of them got very upset with me.

One evening a couple of weeks after I quit the group, my brother and I were sitting in the living room when we heard shaking objects in the kitchen, then the lights went off and on by themselves. I knew something was up, so I decided to go to my room and meditate on what it could be. I sat on the bottom edge of my waterbed facing my dresser and mirror, and then lit a candle. A few seconds later, the window started shaking violently then flew open, blowing the drapes in. Then, the most bizarre thing—the water bed started jumping up and down with me on it! Now when filled with water the bed weighed at least a thousand pounds, so this was really impressive. I thought I was involved in remake of the Exorcist. Remembering what my father taught me, I resolved myself to confront whatever it was with absolutely no fear because I knew that was the only way to approach the situation.

I looked into the mirror on my dresser and saw—to my amazement—the man who was the leader of the band. He acted surprised that I could see him. I gathered all of my strength and said very firmly and loudly "I know who you are and what you want. But you don't know who *I* am. You will leave now and not return ever again." I said this in a very threatening manner. His face faded away and the bed and window stopped moving. My brother came rushing into the room, wondering what the loud noises were and I told him, "Oh, I just got rid of a witch." That band leader never bothered me again.

I have confronted evil spirits at other times and always did so without fear and having total confidence in my ability to stop whatever they were trying to do. There are people in this world and beings not of this world that will try to take advantage of the powers of an inexperienced psychic. When you are open to other worlds, you are open to everything, not just the good stuff. Fortunately, most of the time things are greatly exaggerated in the movies and they don't describe the real world. Most beings are just like you and me and not evil or negative.

There are also reasons why spirits linger in a certain space—sometimes we cannot understand why they choose to stay here, but there may be a reason why they are just not ready to move on yet. As long as the spirit understands fully that their physical body has died, then I feel it is their choice whether or not they move on now or wait until they are ready. In some cases, the spirit feels that they have unresolved issues that they want to communicate to their loved ones.

I worked on a case for a family who was distraught over the sudden death of their mother and apparent haunting of the house. They could not find a copy of her will. I helped them find it by talking to their mother—it was in a hidden safe in the house. I even got the combination of the safe from their mother. After they had the will in their hands all of the haunting activity stopped. Obviously, this was a case of unresolved issues.

The experiences I have had with ghosts have shown me that life does not end with death of the body. All of us live on in spirit, and in fact, the spirit body is what feels more like "home" to a person than the physical body. My guides tell me that the spirit body is made up of light photons; therefore, I suspect that this may be what the orbs are that we and other ghost hunters catch on film.

My guides also say that we may have thousands of lifetimes on earth or on other planets or dimensions, and that it is even possible to experience several "lives" at the same time. I have known since childhood that the spirit reincarnates and that souls tend to stay with the same family groups. This may be why we often feel as if we have had an experience that we couldn't possibly have had in this lifetime or sometimes feel out of sorts like we don't "belong" here. If you spent most of your lifetimes on another planet, then decided to see what it was like on Earth, it is easy to see that you might not feel at home for quite some time.

I have found that people who are unable to communicate with spirits are often afraid to do so. Their fear of the unknown may be what stops them. I think this fear is largely due to influence from movies, other family members, and maybe their church. People's imagination sometimes gets the better of them, and they may believe that all sorts of bad things will happen if someone communicates with a loved one or spirit who has passed on. In most cases, you will not encounter anything negative, however.

If you can be open to spirits of those who have passed to the other side you may find that they will give you assistance and comfort. Even if you are not able to communicate to the extent that I do, don't be discouraged. Try listening a little closer to that "intuition" which may warn you of a dangerous situation or help you out with a problem. That intuition may just be your "guardian angel," who could be your relative. You've heard the old adage, "Practice makes perfect," and this applies to contact with spirits, too. The more often you acknowledge their presence, the more they will help you.

CHAPTER 4

How to Communicate With Ghosts

"O Death, rock me asleep, bring me to quiet rest, let pass my weary guiltless ghost out of my careful breast."

Anne Boleyn

I am often asked how a person can learn to see or communicate with ghosts. If you see a ghost, it probably means two things: that your third eye (psychic center located in the center of your forehead) is open, and also that the spirit probably wants you to see him/her.

Spirits inhabit a higher dimension, and it is my opinion that they either have to lower their vibratory rate, or you have to raise your vibratory rate so you can see them, or it may be a combination of both. That is why it is rare to see a clear apparition or catch one on film. Some photographic and infrared equipment capture pictures of ghosts because the equipment is able to "see" a higher level of vibration than humans can (see the chapter on photographing ghosts).

By "vibratory rate" I mean that you must attain or "tune in" to certain levels of frequency in order to view or experience those things that are also on a higher frequency (such as spirits, elementals, or even UFOs). Raising your vibratory rate — and consciousness — may be accomplished in several ways.

My favorite methods are eating a mostly vegetarian diet, spending time in nature and around water, practicing using my psychic abilities, and meditation— which calms the mind and allows you to concentrate on one thing at a time. I highly suggest taking a course or two on meditation if you don't already know how, but following are some hints on how to get started:

Margie's Meditation Method

Meditation can help you get to the Beta level of consciousness, where psychic abilities are more easily accessed. At the Beta level our brain waves average at around 12—15 cycles per second. At Theta state brainwaves are between 6-7 HZ, and at Alpha (normal waking and relaxed state) brainwaves are between 7 and 12 HZ. Beta level is the state we try to achieve before contacting the other side.

1.) Pick a time to practice every day, preferably at night when it is quiet and there is little activity going on. Try to stick to the same time every day. I meditate just before going to bed.

2.) Pick a place to meditate that is comfortable and where you won't be disturbed by people, pets, or loud noises like traffic or trains.

3.) Sit in an easy chair, or lie down on a bed or couch and use pillows or blankets to get very comfortable. I prefer to lie down because it is more comfortable for me. If you fall asleep while meditating don't worry about it. *Note: Meditation before sleep often allows you to have a deeper, more restful sleep.*

4.) Use of a meditation CD is a good way to get the brain down to beta state fairly quickly. Listen to the music and relax. If you don't have a CD, just listen to your own breathing for a few minutes. I can highly recommend Janalea Hoffman's CD's (see the resource listing)
to help you get to a very relaxed state.

5.) Get relaxed: start at your toes and flex, and then relax your muscles from your feet to the top of your head. Start with the feet muscles, then calves, then thighs, etc. all the way to your neck and head. Go back a couple of times to the jaw and neck areas, since this is the area where people hold the most tension. Take your time and don't rush the process. After using this method for a few months, you'll get very adept at relaxing and won't have to go through the entire process anymore. Your entire body will relax at your suggestion.

6.) Clear your mind. You can do any number of activities at this point, based on what your goals are. If you want to contact a loved one who has passed on, or a spirit who is haunting a house, ask to be in contact with that person. Visualize them standing in front of you. When you have a clear picture, ask the person a question and listen for a response. If you don't succeed at first, keep trying. After several sessions you should be able to hear or "feel" the answer. Be sure to write down everything that happened after you stop meditating.

Another project you may want to do while meditating is to create something. First visualize a blank black curtain in front of you. Then visualize whatever it is you would like to manifest in your life—a loved one who passed on that you would like to communicate with, or money, love, a house, job, travel, health, or whatever you wish. Concentrate on that and say to yourself, "This manifests for me now" or something similar, over and over again until you feel confident that you have created this in your life. Believe that this is happening, and it will happen.

Always use positive words instead of negative words. For instance, say "I am completely healthy" instead of "I don't have arthritis," since the subconscious mind understands only what you are concentrating on.

Start with small things that are easier to obtain before moving on to bigger, more important things. You'll be surprised how your life can change using meditation on a daily basis. Don't be discouraged if you have trouble relaxing and concentrating at first. A lot of people find it very difficult to stop for 15-30 minutes a day after a hectic day.

Your mind has to get used to the change, and it may take a while—but after a few weeks you'll start to feel more confident and it will get easier and easier.

A way to get to "level" faster is to use a meditation CD such as Immrama Insight (www.inrama.org) or one of Janalea Hoffman's CD's (www.rhythmicmedicine.com).

I have been meditating for 35 years, and I strongly believe that it has helped me train my mind to the point that I can instantly go into a trance to do work on investigations or ghost hunting. You will get to the stage where you can have "Dual Consciousness," which means that part of your mind is in a trance state, and part of your mind is fully awake, alert, and communicating with others around you.

HINT: The subconscious mind does not understand "good" from "bad," only that it will manifest what you concentrate on or visualize. Therefore, try to keep the thoughts in mind that you want to have happen, rather than focusing on the negative for better results.

Other ways to raise your level of consciousness and vibratory rate:

- **Eat a vegetarian or mostly vegetarian diet.** The lighter foods will bring your frequency up. It may take a while to take effect if you are a meat eater and your body will go through withdrawals for a while. After a few weeks you won't miss meat at all.

- **Drink very little alcohol.** Alcohol lowers your frequency to very low levels—and actually makes you very vulnerable to attack by mischievous entities. Drink no more than a glass of wine or beer a day. I only have one or two per month.

- **Don't eat too much sugar**– many people experience a literal "buzz" when they have sugar. It really upsets the balance of your system and is quite harmful physically as well as psychically. Also do not use artificial sweeteners—I believe that they have a disruptive vibration.

- **Don't smoke.** You know the physical reasons, but it also dramatically inhibits psychic awareness.

- **Practice dowsing.** Dowsing puts you in contact with your higher self through the lower self, or subconscious, which will assist you with all spiritual matters, including awareness. Check out some books on dowsing or take a dowsing class to get started. See the section on dowsing later in this book.

- **Stop hanging around negative people.** If there are any negative people in your life, consider stopping the relationship. Other than the psychological reasons for staying in a positive environment, negative energies from others bring your own energy levels down.

- **Practice "*seeing*."** There is a certain technique to use in order to see auras, energy, and sometimes ghosts. It is called "*seeing*." The method is to relax the eyes rather than staring hard, and is the opposite of what most people think must be used. By relaxing the eyes, you will be using the rods in the eyes, which are photo-receptor cells used for dim-light vision, rather than the cones, which are responsible for daytime and color vision. If you haven't tried this before, you will be in for a treat. You will see things that you never imagined, most likely starting with electromagnetic energy fields around living things. This method alone may be enough for you to see spirits.

- **Practice telepathy games with other people.** Practice makes perfect with anything, so why not psychic abilities? If you use it all the time you'll get good at it. The QUEST Investigation Group routinely practices using several methods in order to keep sharp and learn new skills. Some of the things we practice are listed on the next page.

    1. The missing person: Have someone go outside and stand somewhere on your property while you stay inside in a location where you can't see out windows or doors. Have the person notify you by walkie-talkie or cell phone that they are in position. Tell them to visualize where they are. Now close your eyes and try to pick up the message from that person—look around and see if you can tell where the location is. At first you may only get colors or shapes. After a while, you may get pretty good at it. This can also be done with objects that you can have someone hide inside or outside the house.

2. Playing cards: Using a set of standard playing cards, have someone else pick out cards and look at them, one at a time, while you write down which card you think it is. To make it easier to start with, just take 5 or 6 cards from the deck to use at one time. Work up to using the entire deck. Try to relax while you are doing this and you'll have better results. Write down the first thing that comes to your mind, and don't "over think" it. Your first impulse is usually the right one.

3. The number game: Have one or more people write down and concentrate on a number between 1 and 10. Write down what you think it is. Do this at least 20 times per session. Taking turns with other people makes it more fun.

4. Use Zener Cards: This is a set of 25 cards used in testing for ESP designed by Karl Zener, a Swiss Psychologist and his associate J.B. Rhine, at Duke University in the 1930's. The cards are designed to test psychic abilities. Each set contains five of each of the following cards: Circle, Square, Three wavy lines, Five-pointed star, and Circle. To use, have someone shuffle the deck and look at a card, while you try to perceive what it is. Keep a record of your tests. It is best if you have a third party write down the findings so the results are accurate and unbiased. A result of 25% or more in accuracy indicates psychic ability.

You can make up other games and tests on your own and use the ones you like the best. It is a good idea to keep a notebook with records of all of your practice sessions so you can see your progress. You'll probably find that your skills will improve over time. The more you practice, the faster the results.

Hypnosis

Hypnosis is a method to access the subconscious mind and communicating with it. Hypnosis can access a deeper level of mind than normal mediation can, and in some cases, the person can go deep enough that the hypnotist is able to communicate with other beings outside the self. This can be useful if trying solve a difficult case, but hardly practical for frequent use.

It might be worthwhile to have several sessions with a certified hypnotist to help you relax and learn how to get in touch with your subconscious mind. For most people, they find it easier to meditate on their own after several hypnosis sessions with a professional. See the Resources section for my recommended hypnotist source.

Sometimes *seeing* ghosts is just a matter of *wanting* to see them. I believe that most places are haunted and there are spirits around us all the time since I see them often, so it is just a matter of finding out what the best technique is for you to be able to communicate with them.

Don't be discouraged if you just can't see anything, however. If you sense there is a presence nearby, use your pendulum and ask questions that way. This is easy to do. Note: See my dowsing techniques later in this book.

How to Communicate With Ghosts Using Your Sixth Sense

After you've practiced some of the techniques mentioned previously, it is time to practice seeing, hearing, or feeling spirits. Using the sixth sense—clairvoyance, clairaudience, and clairsentience—means being able to trust observations that are much more subtle than everyday experiences. The world of the psychic is much different. It is difficult to explain, but once you experience it, you'll know what it is.

Clairsentience is the first intuitive talent that people report having. It means that you sense something without benefit of seeing or hearing it. You just "know" something. This is the first stage of psychic awareness, and is usually called "intuition" by lay-persons. Intuition is associated with persons who know that aunt Betty is going to call on the phone in a few minutes, or that someone is talking about them at that moment. But it can go beyond that to include investigative work such as ghost hunting, and can be used to sense what happened at a location and who is doing the haunting.

The intuitive learns to trust what he sees or hears or feels that is beyond the normal five senses. This is difficult at first, because it may not seem "real." The reality is, however, that intuition *is* real, and it becomes clearer as you practice using these talents. For instance, if you stick your hand in a freezer, you will instantly feel physically cold, but if a spirit passes by you may feel a coldness, or sense a coldness, which in most cases will be much less obvious than the freezer cold. This is one example of the subtleness of the experience.

Clairvoyance is similar, in that you use your third eye, rather than your physical eyes for most of this work. Some people call this technique Remote Viewing. I close my eyes when contacting spirits because I see better that way using my third eye. When I want to see a physical manifestation however, I'll switch to using my physical eyes in the relaxed state mentioned earlier.

When looking with your physical eyes you may see apparitions, fog, mist, orbs, shadows, or shapes. On some investigations I've seen strange shapes appear such as a music stand, a cane, an umbrella, and a ball. All of these things were significant to a particular investigation, and all of them appeared as black shapes, not in color.

Using the third eye is quite different. What you need to see or what is important will appear to you very clearly, in color, with enough light to get a good picture. For me, it is like watching a movie. If I want to go back in time to watch a particular event, I'll often see the location with all of the surroundings, the people present, what they were wearing, etc. However, this method is not 100% accurate when it comes to timing of the event. Time is the absolute hardest thing to get, and any clairvoyant will tell you the same thing. If you ask to go to a particular date, you'll have more luck than if you ask what the date was of an event. This must have something to do with our perception of time. In order to get around this problem, I'll often look around the room I'm visiting for a newspaper or magazine with a date on it and sometimes I'll get lucky.

When in "third eye" mode, the people or spirits I talk with appear alone, usually with no surroundings or distractions. They look very clear to me, but every little detail may not always be apparent unless they want me to see something of importance. It might be important to be able to identify the spirit, so they often show me a tattoo or scar in order for me to be sure I'm talking to the right person.

In order to get to the state of consciousness necessary to use the third eye, I go into what I call a "dual state of consciousness." For me, this means that part of me is fully conscious, and part of me is in a trance-like state. I believe that my years of meditation practice and practice using my psychic abilities every day allows me to do that. For others it may also be very easy to learn how to do, but for some not so easy. I suggest practicing getting to this state of mind in order to become more proficient. Hypnosis sessions seem to speed this along. If you've ever been hypnotized, you may remember the feeling of part of you sinking and letting go, yet having a part of you observe the process at the same time. That observer part is the conscious state.

I simply ask to go to a particular time and place where an event happened that may be important to the case. If possible, I sit in a comfortable recliner, but if not, I can do this standing if it is just for a short time. I have someone with me at all times to record when I'm doing trance work because sometimes I forget what I saw or said, or in some cases, did. This may be a sign of getting older, but I suggest having someone with you or use a recorder in order to have an accurate record of events. When I investigated a suicide in 1985, my hand went into the shape of a gun and I raised it to my temple without knowing it, and the observers around me saw that happen. While I did not "see" what the method of death was at the time, the person had indeed shot himself in the temple.

It is important to be very observant while doing trance work because solving the puzzle may be in the details. Look around at buildings, inside rooms, at paperwork, books, desks, and of course, people. Observe what the people are wearing, how they interact with each other, their facial expressions, and what they do.

The Ghost Hunter's Field Guide

Sometimes you'll be drawn to look at something that your analytical mind wants to ignore, but don't give into that feeling. Go ahead and take a look at whatever it is that you are drawn to because it may be very significant. One case in particular comes to mind, when I was drawn to look at food on the table, then rat poison in the kitchen cabinet. Careful observation of the death of the person indicated that he had indeed been poisoned but that no one knew about it. His spirit lingered because he wanted justice, even though all of the people involved had been long gone. I worked with him and was able to get him to move on.

Clairaudience is simply hearing the other side. Usually, this means hearing the voice of a spirit talking, but can also be the sounds of a plane, traffic, or other things that might be an important part of a message. If a person is trying to communicate that he was killed by a train I may hear a train whistle blowing, or if they were murdered by gun I'll hear the gunshot.

The ability to hear the other side comes in very handy when dealing with the spirit world because the spirits can tell you exactly what happened and why they haunt. I've heard it all —and here are some samples of what the spirits have said on tape and directly to me:

"I was wronged and I want revenge"
"This is my favorite place and I just like to visit."
"This is MY house and everyone needs to get out!"
"This is where I died, and this is where I'll stay."
"I'm looking for my mommy."
"Where is my family?"
"Why can't my family see or hear me?"
"What are you doing in my house?"

"I killed him/her because _____."
"This is none of your business."

When you take the role of the psychic, remote viewer, or intuitive, you also take on the responsibility for communicating with the dead and helping them understand that they have died and nothing can be done about that. You'll want to make them understand that they need to move on with their spirit guides, family, or angels that are waiting for them. If this is something you want to do but are still having trouble with after using the techniques outlined in this book, I suggest taking some classes at your local metaphysical book store, Transcendental Meditation Center, or check online for classes at other locations near you. Large conferences also often have workshops on hypnosis, remote viewing, psychic training, and more. I can recommend Deloris Cannon's hypnosis workshops and certified hypnotists – visit www.ozarkmt.com for more information.

Are You Psychic?

Take this test to see if you can see ghosts now, without any training or practice:

1.) Do you ever have the feeling of being watched when no one is around? yes
2.) Have you ever had a dream that later came true? yes
3.) Do you dream in color and in great detail? yes
4.) Have you ever had a Déjà vu experience? yes
5.) Did you ever know that someone was going to call you, then the phone rang and it was them? yes

The Ghost Hunter's Field Guide

6.) Are you open-minded about the paranormal? yes
7.) Do you meditate? no
8.) Have you ever had a strong feeling about something, such as not to drive a certain way, only to find out later that there was a reason? no
9.) Do you wear black most of the time? yes
10.) Does psychic ability run in your family? NO
11.) Are you more creative/artistic than logical/analytical? yes
12.) Do you have success when dowsing or using a Ouija board or similar device? yes

If you answered yes to seven or more questions above, you are already have some psychic ability, and just need to work on some of the techniques mentioned in this book to expand you mind. A yes answer to all of the above means that you are extremely psychic and are probably already seeing ghosts. If you answered yes to less than seven questions, keep working and your skills will improve as long as you have an open mind.

HINT:

Don't be discouraged if you can't see ghosts—that doesn't mean they aren't there, and it doesn't mean that you can't get evidence with other means.

CHAPTER 5

Ghost Hunting Tools and Techniques

"All houses are haunted. All persons are haunted. Throngs of spirits follow us everywhere. We are never alone."

Barney Sarecky

It is good practice to use scientific means to obtain evidence of ghosts, however, keep in mind that it may take hours, days, or weeks before getting evidence of a haunting using these methods. The ideal investigation would include setting up cameras and voice recorders for a day or a week prior to doing an on-site investigation, in order to get as much evidence as possible, but that is not practical for most weekend ghost hunters. Most of us have full-time jobs and don't have the resources or time needed to do scientific investigations, nevertheless, hobby ghost hunters have gotten some good video, voice, and photographic evidence, not to mention the tactile evidence experienced on the scene.

Following is a list of items and their functions, which can be useful in confirming an anomalous presence. Practicing ghost hunters usually keep their equipment in a "Ghost Hunting Bag", which is always ready to go.

Laser Thermometer: This is a high-tech gadget that my husband uses for his outdoor brick bake oven, and I use in the field when ghost hunting. You just aim it at a surface and pull the trigger to see what the temperature is. Often we will find a drop or rise in temperature in a location where we see or sense a spirit. It is a good device to use to prove that there is something anomalous about an area.

Digital Thermometer: Since a laser thermometer is limited to detecting surface temperature, I also carry a digital thermometer which reads the ambient room temperature. This can be quite useful when a drop in temperature is noted in specific spots in mid-air.

EMF Detector: This handy gadget detects electromagnetic fields around any electronic device but may also "spike" when a spirit is nearby. Be careful to check for any electrical wires or junction boxes, computers, radios, or T.V.'s in the area that may cause high readings. In the absence of any electronics or wiring, you can be reasonably sure that there is another cause for any high readings.

Digital Cameras and Video: We have four digital cameras and one professional Sony HI-8 camcorder, as well as "trip cameras" which get set up in rooms where a lot of activity is suspected. Movement triggers the camera to take a picture and it is totally silent. Just leave it alone after setting up and check the memory card later, and you may be surprised at what the camera picks up.

We have used digital cameras and digital video cameras to get images of orbs, foggy shapes, shadows, and occasionally a spirit. Sometimes things show up on disk that can't be seen with the naked eye. We never manipulate photos except to lighten or darken and add contrast if needed to see objects better.

In an emergency situation you may be able to use a cell phone camera.

Be sure to take along extra charged batteries since it is common for ghosts to drain power sources. I keep my spare batteries in the car, away from the investigation site just in case a ghost drains all of the batteries at the same location at the same time. It is thought that spirits need energy to materialize and take it from the nearest source, which may be your camera batteries.

Motion-Activated Digital Camera: Available online, these inexpensive cameras can be mounted on a wall and take a picture automatically when there is any movement in the area, and with little or no noise. A memory card in the camera can be removed and reviewed later for evidence, and the larger the card, the more photos can be stored. I suggest placing one or more of these cameras in highly active rooms at different heights. You may leave the room in order to investigate other areas. Make sure there are no house pets around that may trip the camera. Both indoor and outdoor motion-activated cameras are available.

Night Vision Monocular or Binoculars: This is a single-or double eye piece device that allows a person to see in pitch darkness or with very little light. We sometimes pick up spirits with it, and then try to take a photo of the same area. Check out hunting gear suppliers for good night vision monoculars. I find it difficult to hold and look through this small view finder for more than a few minutes. Toy stores have new night vision head gear for kids that work very well and are easier to use. These only have a 50-foot range, but for ghost hunting you shouldn't need more than that. You may be surprised at what else you can see with this device— UFO hunters are now using longer range Night Vision gear to see UFO's. Note: never aim the device at a source of light or your retinas could be injured.

Digital Voice Recorder: We use this to capture answers from ghosts. This is commonly known as an EVP (Electronic Voice Phenomena). Someone holds the recorder while asking a question, then pauses to allow time for a spirit to answer. Often when we play back the recorder a ghostly voice will have replied that we didn't hear at the investigation. Sometimes during an investigation I will hear a voice reply to me but others around me don't hear it, then when we play back the recorder others can hear it. Get one that has at least four hours of recording time.

The Ghost Hunter's Field Guide

Wind Meter: Used to measure any breeze inside buildings that may indicate a ghostly presence. Be careful to thoroughly check for any other source of air movement due to fans, open windows and doors, etc. before attributing it to a ghost. Sudden breezes from nowhere may be an indication of ghostly activity.

Pendulums and Dowsing Rods: Pendulums and dowsing rods are very handy to use on an investigation because we can often get immediate answers to yes or no questions or help in guiding us where to go on a site. I always carry a pendulum with me just in case I need it. See "How to Dowse" to learn more about dowsing.

Baby powder, cornstarch or flour: Take along something that you can sprinkle on the floor and leave overnight in a place where there are no people and where reported paranormal activity happens on a regular basis. Sometimes hand or foot imprints will be made in the powder when you return. Be sure that no one can play a hoax by placing a motion-activated digital camera at floor level.

UV Light: We have done some experimenting done using UV lights that are used in HVAC equipment to kill bacteria after I got a telepathic communication from my mother from the other side. She suggested that we would be able to see ghosts better that way. Blacklights have also proved useful for this purpose.

Psychics: Don't forget to take along someone who is clairvoyant! This can be invaluable when trying to determine why a ghost is haunting a place, what they want, and sometimes what their name is and the year they died. After getting this information, you may want to go to the local public library or county clerk's office and see if you can find records that match what you find at the site. Some psychics are able to communicate with spirits and ask them to move on (if that is the desire) or get detailed information that is not obtainable any other way.

White Noise: White noise has been uses successfully to capture disembodied human voices on recorders. Use of a television turned to a channel with no programming, or a radio tuned to a frequency without programming can be used in a pinch. White noise CD's that contain every frequency from 0 Hz to 22,000 Hz are also available. It is thought that ghosts are able to communicate more easily while white noise is played. Try using this method while filming or audio recording the session. Ask questions, then allow time for a response. You may hear responses or the responses may be captured on a recording device. Sometimes ghosts will even ask their own questions!

Wind or Fan: One day I tried this technique after a communication with my mother, who suggested it so that others in the family could hear her speak. We used a small oscillating fan during the first session, and my daughter and I clearly heard my mother's voice call my daughter's name. I have used fans and wind, and even whole-house heating and air conditioning vents with successful results when contacting spirits. If it is windy, go outside and ask questions, then listen to the wind. Also try putting a fan on low speed and stand in front of it, or sit next to a vent in a house while the air conditioning or heat is on. Ask questions and listen carefully. We have received some very clear replies using these methods that everyone on the ghost hunting team can hear. I would call this another "White Noise" method, since noise is produced by the fan.

Communication Device: Bring along a round pencil or short dowel rod, tennis ball, marbles, or other objects that can be easily moved. Place the object on a smooth surface and ask the spirit if it can move the object. If it can, ask it to move in answer to your questions. A "yes" answer indicated by a moving object, and a "no" answer is no movement. Be sure to have your video camera aimed at the object. It is often easier for spirits to communicate in this manner.

Drinking Glass: For a group to use to contact spirits. Useful when used on a smooth-surface table that has been painted with "yes," "no," and/or letters for the spirit to communicate with. The method is to have each person place one finger on the bottom of the overturned glass, ask a question, and wait for an answer. A round table works best.

Make Your Own Ghost Communicator

An inexpensive DIY project

1.) Obtain a 6-foot or longer length of 6" - 8" diameter single wall B-vent chimney pipe (available at hardware stores) or single-wall black chimney pipe.

2.) Place the pipe right in front of a fan. You may need to raise the pipe on some books, or place it on a table with the fan on a chair. Be sure to place the fan setting on non-oscillating. The smaller the fan the better, however, higher fan speeds seem to work better. I don't suggest using CPU Fans because they aren't strong enough.

3.) Place a recorder near the opposite end of the pipe, ask questions and listen carefully. You may be surprised to hear voices clearly from the other side.

CHAPTER 6

How to Dowse for Spirits

"All I'm trying to do is not join my ancestral spirits just yet."

Joshua Nkomo

Dowsing, also known as "water witching" or "divining" is a practice that has been around for thousands of years. It works well to find water or minerals, and for ghost hunting as well. Many people who have learned how to dowse do it on a daily basis to find missing objects, or even to use as a diagnostic tool. After learning how to dowse, you may want to get in the habit of carrying a pendulum with you at all times - you'll be glad to have it with you to use as a tool when you need it.

Who is Answering When You Dowse?

When dowsing, you are in contact with your Higher self, who knows everything and communicates with you through your subconscious or Lower self. The Lower self uses the muscles and energy in and around your body to make a dowsing tool react and give you answers. It does this my moving a pendulum, L-rods, wood Y-rods, or any other dowsing device. In essence, you are talking to yourself when you dowse. If you clear properly (see description following) you will be sure to communicate only with your Lower and Higher self.

Clear First

Always clear yourself and the area before dowsing in order to remove any negativity or thoughts that could confuse the answers you get from the pendulum. Ask to be in contact with your higher self, then ask your higher self to do a clearing. The pendulum will move in a clockwise direction until it is finished, then will stop.

How to Use a Pendulum

You can use any device that is heavy enough to move when

dangled —such as keys, a pendant, or a purchased pendulum made out of stone, crystal, or brass. The higher self seems to be able to communicate easier when using natural materials. I seem to have the best luck with heavier brass pendulums and prefer to use the "UFO" style. I also keep a quartz crystal pendant around my neck that serves double duty for protection and as a pendulum. You might consider wearing a similar type of pendant that can also be used as a pendulum when you need it, or carry a small pendulum in your pocket.

The Pendulum Answers

You can use any directions you like, but the most common method is to ask the pendulum to move in a clockwise direction for a "yes" answer, a counter-clockwise direction to indicate a "no" answer, and straight up and down for a "maybe" or "not quite" answer. You may also want to ask the pendulum to return to these position in-between questions so it is ready to answer quickly.

If desired, you can also ask the pendulum to stop or say "ok" after you get an answer so it will not keep on moving. When first using a pendulum, you should indicate which directions are to mean which answers. In essence, you are telling the pendulum your preferred method of communication.

Asking Questions

It is usually easiest to ask for "yes" or "no" answers to questions, but there are times when you may want to use the pendulum in different ways. If you look on the front of the chart on the next page, there are a set of numbers in an arch shape. If you are looking for a number answer, it is faster to hold the pendulum in the arch area below the numbers and ask it to point in the direction of the number you are looking for. It will start moving in a straight line towards that number. Similarly, you may ask for a yes, no, maybe, or try again later answer by holding the pendulum over the words and waiting for a "yes" clockwise response.

The more you dowse, the better you'll get, and the faster the responses will be to your questions. Try to allot a few minutes a day to dowsing, and you'll have it down in no time. Don't be discouraged if at first you don't get immediate answers—the pendulum needs to warm up to your energies and your subconscious and higher self need to get used to the idea that you wish to contact them on a regular basis.

How to Use Dowsing Rods

Dowsing rods or "L-Rods" are used differently than a pendulum. Most dowsers use rods when looking for something like water or minerals, but they can be used to send you in the direction of anything, including ghosts. Some dowsing rods have witness chambers in them on the ends where you can place an item that is the same thing you are looking for, i.e. gold or silver. For ghost hunting, however, the witness chamber is not practical to use. Dowsing L-Rods have a handle with a hole drilled in it to allow the rod to move freely.

Hold the dowsing rods in your hands and place your thumb over the top of the movable part to stead it until you are ready to start dowsing. Hold the rods at a 90-degree angle to your body. Now think about what you want to find and ask a question such as "If there is a ghost here, where is it?" You should feel a pull on the rods, which will usually move to the right or left, then straighten out when you are headed in the right direction, and then pull you towards the ghost or whatever you are looking for. The rods will then cross over each other when you are in the right spot.

The pull of energy can be quite strong at times, especially for experienced dowsers. I believe this has to do with the energy exchange between the dowser and the rods. In order to get an accurate reading, keep your mind focused on the object you are searching for and try to keep distractions to a minimum when you are first learning to do this. You may want to practice searching for different things for a couple of weeks for car keys or items people can hide for you before using the rods as a ghost hunting tool. I also find the rods useful for finding gravestones or locating where a fellow ghost hunter is on the scene.

HINT: Practice dowsing every day and in a few weeks it will be second nature.

How to Make Your Own Wood Divining Rod

1. Traditionally, dowsers cut a forked branch from a willow or apple tree, but you can use any branch available.
2. Trim away leaves or twigs.
3. Trim the branch so that each arm of the "Y" is equal in length and is approximately two feet long.
4. The remaining part of the branch should be just a few inches in length.
5. To use, hold your palms up with one part of the "Y" in each hand. Keep the rod parallel to the ground and do not hold the arms close to the body. Walk over the area you are searching while keeping the item in mind that you are seeking. When you arrive at the spot the rod will move strongly down (or sometimes up), indicating the location of the item (or ghost) you are looking for.

HINT: In a pinch, use wire hangers for dowsing by placing one wire hanger in each hand, long side in the palm, with the hooked end pointed down.

How to Make Your Own Clay Pendulum

1. Purchase polymer clay and 6" length of wide (1/4" - 3/8") silver jewelry chain at a craft store.
2. Following instructions on the label, condition clay, then form in to a 2" length that is 1/2" wide at the top and tapers to a point at the bottom
3. Insert a wire loop in the top, or make a loop out of clay and attach it to the top.
4. Make a small 1/2" diameter ball of clay and insert a wire loop in one end, leaving enough space to attach the chain to later.
5. Bake the clay as directed and let cool.
6. Connect the purchased chain to the ball and pendulum.
7. Hold on to the ball portion and allow the pendulum to hang freely when dowsing.

Use the dowsing assistant on the next page, make your own, or use a Ouija board if desired. Be sure to clear first to remove any negative energy.

Pendulum Dowsing Assistant

NO **MAYBE** **YES**

A B C D E F G H I J K L M N
O P Q R S T U V W X Y Z

CHAPTER 7

Photographing Ghosts

"Humans are amphibians - half spirit and half animal. As spirits they belong to the eternal world, but as animals they inhabit time."

C. S. Lewis

The Ghost Hunter's Field Guide

This is probably the most frustrating part of ghost hunting. A picture is the evidence that most of us want to get as proof of a spirit's existence. Yet invariably, we don't have a camera available when we see something, or when we don't see anything we don't use the camera.

I encourage you to take photos of nothing. Just take pictures of everything around you, even aim the camera behind your head while you are facing forward. You'll be pleasantly surprised at what may show up in photos taken with any type of camera, when you may not have seen anything unusual at the time you took the picture. And if you do sense that there is something in the area, by all means snap some pictures.

Take your still camera or video camera with you everywhere, and when you get the chance, or have a feeling that there may be spirits in the area, snap some pictures. I carry a small Sony pocket camera that is thin and lightweight enough to carry in my purse all the time, and it takes 14 megapixel photos! The technology is amazing and the prices are very reasonable.

With digital cameras you can easily delete any photos that don't show anything so you don't waste money on printing.

You might want to get out your old photo albums and start thumbing through them to see if there is anything anomalous that you may have missed. Orbs, mist, fog, and apparitions have shown up on some of our 35mm, old Polaroids and newer digital photographs that we missed before we were actually looking for anything odd. It is also a fact that unless you are looking for anomalies you may miss them altogether!

The Ghost Hunter's Field Guide

(Brightness increased in order to see orbs better)

This is a photo taken of an area where we sensed spirits near a stream. I've seen the ghost of an old prospector from the early to mid 1800's here whenever we visit the park. While in a "Dual Consciousness" state I viewed the area and saw a tent with a fire in front of it, and the man panning gold in the stream and tending his cook pot over the fire. The man does not like people to bother him and he still hangs out at his "claim" many years later. Note several orbs in the picture.

There are no orbs in other photos taken before or after these in the same location with the same camera. So that means that within a few seconds, something anomalous possibly appeared. It is a good idea to take lots of pictures of the same location for this reason. See the full investigation story of this site later in this book.

The Ghost Hunter's Field Guide

Three unknown lights *Streetlight in far background*

Note: the camera must have moved while the shutter was open, causing the streaks of light.

This very unusual photo was taken at a park during a ghost hunting expedition. No one saw any of the three lights at the left at the time the photo was taken but after they showed up on the computer, two of us returned to the exact same spot at the same time of night and could find no sources of light that could explain it. The light at the right is a streetlight in the park. Notice the white blurry light coming from the street light just outside the upper left corner of the photo. The light streaks are extremely bright even though this was on a foggy night. When I took this photo I sensed a lot of activity in the area and felt something watching me but did not see anything with the naked eye.

The Ghost Hunter's Field Guide

Another example of a photographic anomaly is in picture of Kent Dicus of Kansas City standing by the grave of his great-great-aunt, Mary "Mollie" Thomas Dobyns DeHaven at the Walnut Grove Cemetery in Boonville, MO on August 10, 2002.

Kent and his friend, Michael (the photographer) did not see anything out of the ordinary at the time of their visit to the cemetery, however, after developing this photograph they noticed a profile of a person's face behind the grave marker just to the right of Kent.

Neither man has any idea what this clear apparition could be. There is no way a person could stand behind the cross without being seen. Kent and Michael have returned to the same location several times to see if they could find an explanation for this, but have been unable to find anything out of the ordinary.

Also note what appears to be a stream of energy above the column-like marker in the upper right of the picture.

Spirit Fog

Spirit Fog during a Native American ceremony. Photo courtesy of Dennis Kindle

The fog is approximately 14" in diameter, however its height is unknown since it was not visible at the time the photo was taken. Note the zigzag formations in the center. The dark line to the right may be a young tree.

The Ghost Hunter's Field Guide

The photograph above was taken right after a ghost hunt at a local park. Two of us sensed a presence in the area and took several pictures with digital cameras. Most of the photos showed nothing unusual, but this one has an orb in the picture.

There is no orb in other photos taken before or after these in the same location. So that means that within a few seconds, something anomalous showed up. It is a good idea to take lots of pictures of the same location for this reason.

See the full investigation story later in this book.

HINT: Always get permission from landowners or business owners before ghost hunting on their property.

The Ghost Hunter's Field Guide

This photo was taken in my sister-in-law's garden (we call it the "Fairy Garden") on a clear day with no fog present. The fog was not visible to the eye. This area is where small balls of light have been spotted.

Apparition in a field. *Courtesy of Rich Carter*

CHAPTER 8

Good Places to find Ghosts

ı ı

"I cannot but think that it would be a great step if mankind could familiarize themselves with the idea that they are spirits incorporated for a time in the flesh re spirits incorporated for a time in the flesh."

Catherine Crowe

The Ghost Hunter's Field Guide

There are lots of places that are haunted. Besides the obvious graveyards, old forts, historic buildings, Colonial and Victorian homes, there are many other places to look.

One late afternoon I "turned on" my third eye while driving, just to see how many places harbor ghosts in my neighborhood in Independence, Missouri. I drove around the Independence Square, and down Lexington and Short streets, down Winner Road and then Sterling. I was amazed at how many spirits inhabit the houses— in fact, probably 80% of the homes had a ghostly presence. Most were ghosts of elderly people who had lived in the homes. Some were younger people who lived in the houses or on the land before there were any buildings here. I saw a few Native Americans and people dressed in early 1800's attire, as well as Confederate and Union soldiers and nurses.

The location or structure does not need to be very old to have ghostly inhabitants. It is more likely for a spirit to haunt a location that it last knew in life, so this could be its home or the spot where it died, or both.

We have an 11-year old little girl ghost in my house that died during the 1970's. The girl liked to give our visitors a shock by appearing as a solid person to them then fading out. I think she liked to play pranks. I contacted her and she knows she died, but she likes the house and feels comfortable there. I told the girl she could stay if she did not scare anyone else and she hasn't for over 10 years now. The same thing could happen in any home, so don't rule out newer structures.

Also check out parks, abandoned buildings, bridges, old hospitals, mental institutions, old jails and prisons, hotels, restaurants, railroad stations and tracks, churches, battlegrounds, old courthouses, old town squares, places where ghost ships have been seen off of the coast (Florida is a great place for clipper ship sightings) and ghost towns.

Brick buildings seem to be good places to look for some reason. I recently found that the stateroom on a cruise ship we took to the Caribbean was haunted. The ghost made strange fluttering and whispering noises for two nights, and then I saw a dark apparition walk across the room on the night before we went home. Even though the cruise ship is only eight years old, there have been thousands of people on and off the ship, so chances are that a few have died on it and on other cruise ships, too.

Indian burial grounds or sacred spaces may be tempting to investigate, but I prefer to leave them alone out of respect. However, if a house has already been built on the site and the owners are having problems, I do go to see if I can help or refer them to a Native American Shaman. Sometimes communicating with the spirits can alleviate aggressive (Protective) activity. See ghost clearing techniques later in this book.

There are haunted places in every city, town, and county in the U.S., but the older sites seem to have more activity. I've also have good luck in Europe and the U.K. where the structures there are much older and they have a longer history.

Be sure to be very safe and always take a flashlight, water, and a cell phone with you when ghost hunting. It is not a good idea to go to a scary place alone, so always take at least one buddy with you. Also be sure not to damage any property while you are hunting.

CHAPTER 9

The Investigation Process

Interview Witnesses
Rule out Other Possibilities
Get Evidence of a Haunting
Get Rid of Ghosts if Desired

"Behind every man now alive stand 30 ghosts, for that is the ration by which the dead outnumber the living."

*Arthur C. Clarke, 2001:
A Space Odyssey*

The Ghost Hunter's Field Guide

Interview Witnesses

If you are doing serious ghost hunting and want to be very professional about it or plan to write an article or book about your experiences, one of the most important things you can do is to interview witnesses. Talk to people who are currently occupying a home or building, and see if you can locate previous owners as well.

Talk to managers and employees if you can (on your dime). It's a nice gesture to take someone to lunch for the interview if you have time. This information will give you a good idea of what you are dealing with. Be sure not to lead the witness -i.e. make suggestions during the interview.

An example of a leading question would be: "Was the apparition you saw very dark and non-transparent?" Instead, ask "What did the apparition look like?"

Following are some questions I take with me on a clipboard when doing interviews. You might want to copy this and keep several copies with you at all times so you won't forget anything.

1.) What is your name (and other witnesses)?

2.) Address of this location:

3.) When did you first occupy this location?

4.) What types of paranormal activity have you witnessed here?

5.) Sounds: []Talking []Whispering []Footsteps []Singing []Typing []Bells []Door closing/opening []Yelling []Crying []Other

The Ghost Hunter's Field Guide

6.) Smells: []Cigar []Pipe []Cigarette []Perfume []Cologne []Flowers []Foul odor []Firewood smell []Burning house []Other _____

7.) Taste: []Blood []Food []Other
_____

8.) Do you know of any deaths that occurred here?

9.) Do you know the names of any deceased persons?

10.) Is the paranormal activity limited to certain areas?

11.) What unusual things have you seen?
[]Fog []Mist []Orb(s) []Lights []Full apparition(s) []Partial apparition(s) []Solid person []Person faded out and disappeared []Other_____

12.) If voices are heard, are they []male []female []child []baby

13.) Have you seen any animal ghosts?

14.) Have you had any UFO sightings in this area?

15.) Have you had any UFO encounters?
(People who have had UFO sightings often also have "haunted" houses)

16.) Have you witnessed any objects moving? []dropping

The Ghost Hunter's Field Guide

[]thrown []levitating []pulling covers off people
[]Other _____

17.) If so, what were the objects?

18.) Were any of the movements threatening to any member of the family?

19.) Has anyone been physically touched by a ghost?

20.) If so, who was touched and what happened?

21.) Has anyone felt: []a change in temperature in any location []hotter []colder []cold chills/goose bumps []something moving through them []other
_____

22.) Has activity increased over time?

23.) Do your guests/clients notice anything abnormal, or do things happen only around the occupants?

24.) Is there any history about this place? []Fire []Murder []Other
_____

25.) Do you know of any graveyards nearby?

26.) Do you feel a sense of []Calm []Dread []Fear []Uneasiness []Curiosity []Anger when ghosts are around?

27.) Are you or is anyone in your family psychic or intuitive?

28.) If so, have you ever seen ghosts at other locations?

29.) Does activity heighten around any certain time or event?

30.) Has the paranormal activity caused you to
[]sleep poorly []want to move away []stay away as long as possible doing other activities []divorce your spouse []argue

31.) Have any ghosts followed you *to* other locations?

32.) Do you think the ghost(s) followed you *from* another location?

33.) Have you had ghostly activity at other locations you have lived/worked?

34.) Have any spirits been physically violent?

35.) Do they play mischievous tricks like hiding objects and returning them later?
[]Keys []Jewelry []Watches
Other _____

36.) Has anything disappeared from your home/business only to show up at a different location at a later date?

37.) Do any spirits answer you out loud when you ask questions?

38.) Have you heard any audible replies on a digital voice recorder?

38.) Have your utilities: water, electricity, or gas been affected?

Steps of the Investigation Process

1. Do a clearing and protection session using a pendulum, crystal, meditation or affirmations before entering the property.

2. Discuss the haunting with witnesses and fill out the interview form.

3. Survey the grounds during daylight hours if possible to get a feel for the area first, especially if going into an unfamiliar location. Check for hazards like holes in the ground, rocks, etc. that could cause someone to trip or get injured. Mark these areas with a flag or other item that will be noticed.

4. Check for possible normal explanations for activity, sounds, or lights during the day and again at night. Check electrical lines and devices for abnormal EMF readings, check water pipes, pets, wind, open windows, air conditioner or heating vents.

5. Assign jobs and set up equipment on the site. I like to use as much wireless equipment as possible to avoid tripping on wires and the hassle of plugging in equipment in people's homes. We send people out in groups of two so that no one is alone, for safety, and also if something does happen worth noting there is another witness in the same location.

6. Do a walk-through each room with audio and video recorders, ask questions and wait for answers. Be patient. Ask if there are any spirits present, who they are, and what they want. Basically, you can get most of the information you need with those three questions.

Take lots of photos.

7. If you feel cold spots or have other indications of a presence, ask the ghost to move a ball or pencil or other object, or make a noise to indicate their willingness to communicate. Ask yes or no answers, and ask the spirit to answer "yes" by moving an object. If that doesn't work, ask questions with a recorder on to check later, or leave the recorder on all the time to catch answers.

8. Do a trance session with a medium if possible to get more information. Detailed answers may be obtained using this method. Mediums all work differently, so get familiar with how they like to work before having them go on an investigation with you. Some may do remote viewing and don't need to visit the site in order to gain information.

9. Tear down equipment and pack up. Do a second clearing and affirmation with the intention that all spirits will remain where they are now. The reason is that you don't want any pesky spirits following you home.

10. Check film and recorders for evidence after you are rested. Collect all of the evidence saved by each researcher.

11. If warranted, check civil records, newspapers, and libraries for more information about the location.

12. Make out your final report and keep a file of each of your investigations.

The Ghost Hunter's Field Guide

WARNING: Never take children or teens on a ghost hunt. Children are more afraid of ghosts than they usually let on, and possession by an unfriendly spirit is more likely in children than adults. Possession is rare, but it is worth taking precautions against it to start with. Also some spirits have followed children home to haunt them instead of the people at the original place. When this happens it is usually a child ghost who wants a friend, but evil entities can masquerade as children, too.

Rule out Other Possibilities

A professional ghost hunter will always rule out other possibilities for strange phenomena first. By being the skeptic, you will find that often a simple explanation can be found for many claims of hauntings.

Electrical Interference

EMF (Electro-magnetic field) readings can indicate the presence of a spirit. However, always check for obvious and hidden wiring, electrical junction boxes, and conduit that may be running through walls, under floors, or in ceilings. Check electrical switches and outlets, even if the owner believes they are disconnected. In several instances we have found old knob and tube wiring that was hot, even though the owners had the entire house rewired by an electrician. This can give you false positive readings.

Other items in the home that have electro-magnetic fields are electric blankets, alarm clocks, water bed heaters, cordless razors, computers, television sets, and cell phones, to name a few.

Also check outside the structure for nearby overhead or buried power lines or transformers. You'd be surprised how far away you can get EMF readings from these objects. Exposure to electromagnetic fields is a controversial topic. Some scientists believe that EMFs are responsible for brain tumors, cancer, miscarriages and other health problems, as well as a cause of hallucinations. If you get high EMF readings above .05 mG, this may be a source to question.

A Gauss is a common unit of measurement of magnetic field strength. A Gauss (EMF) meter is an instrument which measures the strength of magnetic fields. Inside the Gauss meter there is a coil of thin wire. As a magnetic field radiates through the coil, it induces a current, which is amplified by the circuitry inside the Gauss meter.

Gauss meters can vary in the strength of the magnetic field they are capable of measuring. Since we are using a consumer grade EMF meter to help in our search for ghosts, the accuracy will not be that of a professional meter used by engineers, but will serve our purposes.

When ghost hunting, any EMF readings that occur away from electrical sources should be noted as possible evidence of a haunting.

Noise Sources

The most common complaint from people who think they have a haunted building is odd noises. The noises may sound like creaking floors and stairs, water dripping, scratching, banging, etc. The professional investigator will look for a natural explanation first such as leaking pipes, air in the water lines (this can be very loud), wind, heating/cooling vents that expand and contract when heated or cooled, and animals walking about the house. Wood stove pipes sometimes make noise when in use.

Also look for signs of rodents, squirrels, or raccoons, which can get inside the house through small holes, or under eaves and through chimneys. A common place for squirrel nests is in the attic. Raccoons, bats, squirrels, insects and chimney swifts find that chimneys are an ideal home for them, and we often find that these creatures can make a great deal of noise.

Note: have the homeowner call a licensed animal removal company to get rid of pests—never attempt this on your own. Animals carry rabies and other diseases that you don't want to be exposed to. Also never open a damper to investigate a chimney— you could expose yourself to carcinogenic soot and dangerous disease carrying bird droppings, etc. Not to mention that a live animal could come through the damper into the house.

Light Sources

If the occupant is seeing lights at night, see if you can visit at the time they experience it so you can see what the lights look like. Car headlights are the most common source, but train lights, reflections in windows, helicopters, lighted signs, and street lights should be investigated.

Hallucinations

Although we have rarely encountered a client who hallucinates, you cannot rule out the possibility. Certain medications, some illegal drugs, and some mental conditions may cause hallucinations. Since we are not trained in mental health we never mention this to the client. However, there are some cases where this might be the source of ghost sightings, especially if there is no other evidence and no other witnesses.

Psychic Awareness

I mention this because we have encountered several clients who are very psychic, but had absolutely no training in the area, and had no idea how to handle what they were seeing. Many psychics do not have the ability to turn their third eye (psychic center) off and on at will. They need to gain control of this and get training from another experienced psychic in order to deal with it.

One of the clients I worked with was very psychic and was seeing elementals around her house but had no idea what they were and thought they were ghosts. The elementals were tree spirits and possibly fairies. They moved about the inside and outside of the home as a tiny ball of bright white/blue light. Sometimes they would manifest in the form of a tiny person. I found that case highly unusual, since most psychics work for years to get to the level of ability to see the things this client could see with no training at all.

Pranks

If you do not find evidence of a haunting, consider that the source may be a prank by other people living in the house, or from neighbors, friends, etc. A case I worked on many years ago turned out to be a teenager in the neighborhood who threw rocks at the house at night after the husband left for work. This is always a possibility.

After your ghost-hunting session if you want more information about the location that the homeowner can't provide, do research on your own. Libraries usually have micro-film of local newspapers and civil records offices will have copies of deeds and plat maps that may be useful. Also be sure to check old obituary pages for information about the deceased if applicable.

Your county Historical Society may have records that are not available elsewhere, and of course, the internet is a good resource, especially for news articles that are fairly recent. I've also used Ancestry.com for many of our investigations because they have access to many online resources such as military records and census records; however, there is a fee to join.

The Paranormal Investigation Report

This report form is a sample of what I use in the field, and then we enter the evidence into a computer that is used just for this purpose. Sometimes we take the computer with us in the field and one person does entry on site in order to save time. If you are very serious about ghost hunting, there are some programs available that will allow you to keep audio, video, and still photos in the report. A report will also assist in making you look more professional. In any case, keep some kind of record of your investigation for future reference and provide the client with a copy. I also keep a copy on a CD in case of a computer crash. Copy the following or revise it to suit your needs.

Date_____
Site_____
Owner _____
Address_____
Allowable access times_____
Phone_____Cell_____
Emergency contact_____
Time:_____to_____
Temperature outside: _____ Inside:_____
Moon cycle: []Full []New []Waxing or Waning []no moonlight
Weather conditions: (wind, rain, snow, clouds, etc._____

Lead Investigator: _____
Investigators: _____
_____
_____
Guests: _____

The Ghost Hunter's Field Guide

Equipment used and investigator assigned:
Digital camera_____
Video camera_____
Night vision equipment_____
Audio equipment_____
Ambient Thermometer_____
Laser Thermometer_____
Infra red camera:_____
EMF Meter: _____
White Noise: _____
Walkie-talkies:_____
Other: _____

Unmonitored equipment set up and location:
Indoor motion-activated still cameras:_____
Outdoor motion-activated still cameras: _____
Remote wireless cameras connected to computer: _____
_____
Computer (command center):_____
Other:_____

Events experienced by each investigator: (describe in detail)
Lead Investigator:
Sound _____
Taste_____
Touch/feeling_____
Smell_____
See_____
_____

Investigator 1:
Sound _____
Taste_____
Touch/feeling_____
Smell_____
See_____
_____

The Ghost Hunter's Field Guide

Investigator 2:
Sound _____
Taste _____
Touch/feeling _____
Smell _____
See _____

Investigator 3:
Sound _____
Taste _____
Touch/feeling _____
Smell _____
See _____

Investigator 3:
Sound _____
Taste _____
Touch/feeling _____
Smell _____
See _____

Homeowner: (if participating)
Sound _____
Taste _____
Touch/feeling _____
Smell _____
See _____

Guest:
Sound _____
Taste _____
Touch/feeling _____
Smell _____
See _____

The Ghost Hunting Kit

All serious ghost hunters need to have a ghost hunting kit that is ready to go at a moment's notice. I use a black duffle bag with outside pockets on it for small things. If you keep everything in one place you'll never be looking for stuff before you go on a hunt. Pack these items in your bag:

Flashlights with red gel coverings so you can see in the dark but not be blinded (available at Wal-Mart)
Note pads and pens
Digital recorders
Digital camera
Motion-activated camera(s)
Video camera
EMF detector
Spare batteries for everything
Crystals for protection and communication
Night vision goggles or monocular
Night vision camera
Compass
Walkie-talkies
Chairs to sit on if doing outside work
Mosquito repellant
First aid kit

And don't forget to take your cell phone!

How to Get Rid of Ghosts

Before considering asking spirits to leave a place, think about what would happen if they were gone. Are ghosts good for business in a hotel or restaurant? If so, the owners may not want the spirits to leave. If the spirit likes being in a location, are they hurting anyone by being there? If not, maybe the best thing to do is to leave them alone. However, if the ghost is scaring people and you need to get rid of it there are a few methods that have worked well for me.

The first method is to simply ask the ghost to leave. That may sound too simple, but it usually works. You may want to talk to it and explain why by saying "You are scaring us," or "This is _____'s house and she is not comfortable having you here.", then calmly ask it to go away. If this doesn't work right away, try talking in a firmer voice without yelling or getting angry. Anger only gives more power to negative spirits

As I mentioned earlier, ghosts may not be aware that they are dead so you may have to explain to them that they are no longer part of the physical world and that they should look around for their spirit guide and move on towards the light. I close my eyes and visualize then going into the light. This method has been very successful for me. Some spirits are reluctant, but if you tell them that it will be better for them this way, they eventually move on.

If the spirit simply refuses, try not giving it any attention or talking about it at all. This takes energy away from the spirit. Don't show any fear, because the energy of fear empowers negative spirits. Also do not use a Ouija board or have anything to do with the supernatural, which could open doors to the spirit world and allow the spirit more access during the time you are trying to get it to leave and until you are certain it is gone.

Sample of a Real Ghost Extraction

Sometimes ghosts will appear in the least likely places. Claudia Green and George Miles from Kansas City asked me to assist them in getting a ghost to leave them alone.

Just the week before contacting me the ghost of their friend had appeared in the rear-view mirror of their car—apparently sitting in the back seat- as they were passing by the spot where the friend had died in a car accident exactly one year before. The ghost of their friend had appeared to them as a full body apparition, and had been sitting on their beds leaving an indentation in the covers, speaking out loud, and physically touching their arms.

After I contacted the spirit of their deceased friend during a trance session, I tested her to see if I was indeed speaking to the correct person. She told me to tell her friends that she always wore her signature blue eye shadow, and they confirmed that it was indeed the correct spirit since their friend was known for her blue eye shadow.

It turned out that the spirit was just trying to give the two friends comfort, and was still on the earth plane because Claudia and George kept saying things like "I wish she wasn't gone," and "I wish she were here." Naturally, the ghost of their friend was trying to comfort them, not scare them, and was in fact, just doing what they asked.

I asked if the two were ready to let her go, then I told the spirit of their friend to go with her spirit guides to the light. She did and has not returned since.

CHAPTER 10

How to Protect Yourself While Ghost Hunting

"It is on the acceptance or rejection of the theory of the Unity of all in Nature, in its ultimate Essence, that mainly rests the belief or unbelief in the existence around us of other conscious beings besides the Spirits of the Dead."

H. P. Blavatsky

The Ghost Hunter's Field Guide

In order to protect yourself from mischievous or malicious spirits or worse, and psychic attack during ghost hunting you need to take several steps, some of which need to be done before arriving at the site you want to investigate. Do not forget this step or you could have some unpleasant experiences.

White Light

White light is used for protection by many people. First, get everyone together that is going on the hunt, preferably at a meeting place that is not near the site or at the least before entering the site. Have everyone form a circle and visualize white light above, below, and all around them, forming a protective cocoon of light. White light repels negative energies. Say the following or something similar out loud:

"I repel all negativity from us and this site we are about to visit and call in protective white light to surround us." You may want to repeat this several times.

Upon arrival at the site or after your ghost hunt, you may want to get out your pendulum and do a clearing while visualizing white light (see the dowsing chapter). If at any time during the investigation process you feel threatened, take out your pendulum and do a clearing or repeat the white light protection method.

Some people carry clear quartz crystals with them on ghost hunts, since they carry high energy that negativity can't stand to be around. You might want to wear a crystal pendulum necklace or just carry one in your pocket. You may also charge a particular crystal for protection (see next page).

Wear Black

Another method of protection is to wear black. This may sound like the opposite of what you would expect, but <u>black is a very powerful repellant of negative energy and also gives you more power</u>. <u>Black obsidian works well, too, if carried on your person</u>. <u>If you are doing a lot of ghost hunting, you may want to further protect yourself by keeping crystals in your house all of the time to repel any energies that you might accidentally bring back with you</u>.

Although it is unusual for an entity to follow you home, it can happen. <u>This usually happens to the inexperienced investigator</u>. If you suddenly notice that you are feeling unwell, have extreme fatigue, or poltergeist activity in your house, do an immediate clearing of your home and do the white light visualization daily until you feel better.

Quartz Crystals

It is a good idea to keep a quartz crystal with you for protection; however, it should be cleansed and charged first. Choose a crystal that is a size you can easily carry. You may also want to have extra crystals or clusters in your home to use for protection 24 hours a day.

Obtaining Crystals

I go to Arkansas once a year to dig for my own crystals. It is a very inexpensive way to get your own crystals and assure that they have never been used by others. For a small fee, you bring your own bucket and tools with you to dig in the clay for crystals. Some mines allow you to go to the mine location, and others allow you to dig in piles they bring up for you. We go to the Ron Coleman Mine where the crystals are dug up with bulldozers and placed on the ground at the top of the hill so it is easier to access.

Be sure to wear old clothing and shoes since the red clay stains easily. Bring a crowbar, claw hammer, and a sledge hammer if you are ambitious. I bring my husband with me to do that hard work. You will find small crystals, small and large clusters, and big crystals. Sometimes there are crystals in plain sight, but most of the time you need to dig into the clay with your hands in order to feel them. Wash them off with the water nearby, or take along an extra bucket of water to rinse them in. You are allowed to stay all day to dig for one price.

I have found lots of crystals that I use to place around my entire house inside and out for protection. I also use some for communicating with spirits.

Cleansing a Crystal

I use two methods to cleanse. Either leave the crystal in a bowl of sea salt, Kosher sea salt for one week, or rinse it under cool spring water—preferably under a waterfall, but if none is available use spring water from a jug. This process removes any energy that the crystal may have picked up on its way to you.

Charging a Crystal

Charge crystals with the task you wish to use them for better results. Charge a clean crystal by holding it upside down with the bottom of the crystal in the palm of your hand. Now visualize white light energy coming through the top of your head, down your

The Ghost Hunter's Field Guide

arm, and into the crystal, charging it along with the message to protect you at all times, or to help you communicate with spirits, etc. Do this for several minutes while you are in a quiet place with no interruptions. Stop when you feel that the crystal is fully charged. Only use the crystal you have charged for one purpose. Label your crystals if necessary to keep them separate.

Now keep the crystal in a bag in your pocket or around your neck as a necklace. You may make it into a piece of jewelry if it is the right size and wear it that way. I wire-wrap some of my crystals, which double as an emergency pendulum for cleansing an area if needed.

Periodically re-cleanse and re-charge your crystal and only use this particular crystal for one purpose—protection. You may charge other crystals with different intents (such as communication) if you wish.

Using Crystals

To use crystals for protection from psychic attack, keep one on your person at all times. Take along a crystal pendulum to use as a clearing device when you encounter negative energies at a haunted site. See the section on Dowsing for tips on clearing with a pendulum. Finally, place crystals or clusters around your home for 24 hour protection.

To use a crystal for communication purposes, hold it in your hand and concentrate on the crystal and the spirit you wish to talk with. The communication will usually be telepathic rather than audible, however, keep the digital recorder on because sometimes EVP's come through during communication sessions.

Obsidian

One of my favorites, obsidian is a black smooth volcanic glass stone that is known for its protective qualities. I prefer to keep a 3" diameter round obsidian stone in my house and periodically cleanse it with sea salt. The obsidian stone has the unique quality of absorbing negative energy and keeping it in its external energy field until it is cleansed. Negative energy is drawn to it like a magnet, keeping the negativity away from you or others in the house. To cleanse, simply place the rock in a bowl of sea salt for two days, or wash under running spring water. When you sense that it is clear of any negativity, put it back in its regular place.

I also carry small obsidian with me when doing any kind of investigation work for extra protection. Between my all black clothes, crystal necklace, and the black obsidian, I don't think it's possible for anything negative can get through!

Other stones that are commonly used for protection and usually worn in the form of jewelry are Hematite, Black Tourmaline, Tiger Iron, Bulls Eye Agate, Rainbow Obsidian, Carnelian Agate, Ruby, Andulasite, Blue chalcedony, and Silver. See the next page for a listing of the most common stones used for protection purposes.

Stones with Protection Qualities

Agate: Protects against the Evil Eye
Amber: Protection from evil
Aquamarine: Protects sailors at sea
Blue chalcedony: Protects against evil magic, evil spells
Fluorite Psychic protection
Hematite: Protects the warrior
Labradorite: Protects the aura from energy leakage
Obsidian: Absorbs negative energy
Malachite: General strong protection
Mother of Pearl: Protects newborns
Peridot: Protects the entire body, demon protection
Riverstone: Burial protection
Ruby: Protects family and possessions
Red Jasper: Protects in dangerous situations
Riverstone: Burial and building protection
Silver: Protects for evil spirits
Smoky Quartz: Protects from negativity in healing work
Sunstone: Protects from destructive forces
Tourmaline: Black, is a powerful protector
Turquoise: Protects from injury
Zircon: Protects from bodily harm

For more information on stone properties and uses, just Google the stone's name.

CHAPTER 11

Real Ghost Hunts

"The chief difficulty which prevents men of science from believing in divine as well as in nature Spirits is their materialism."

H. P. Blavatsky

Following are some accounts of ghost hunting investigations completed by the QUEST Investigation Group team, and my own experiences in some of the houses I've lived in. All of my houses have been haunted—you might say that *I'm* haunted. This is something I hear a lot from other psychics, too, so I've come to the conclusion that most houses do have spirits.

My Haunted House

Naturally I can't print the address here or we'd have tourists stopping by every day— but my home is located in an older section of Independence, Missouri. The house is 2500 square feet and consists of an older portion that was built in 1929 and a newer, larger addition that was built in 1986. We did extensive remodeling of the house which included removal of walls and relocation of the lower level bathroom, the addition of a dormer, and expansion of the kitchen. The original floor plan is pretty much the same, however, plus the addition.

Ghosts

From the time we moved in this house in 1987 until the year 2000, my husband and I operated a service business out of our home and had a secretary come in every weekday. The older front living room was converted to an office. My two daughters, ages ten and eight at the time, first brought ghostly activity to my attention when they reported hearing footsteps on the staircase to their bedroom. Sure enough, we heard a man's heavy stomping with boots and a woman's lighter heels on the steps.

When people visiting heard the steps and asked about it we said "Oh, that's just one of the ghosts." I decided to do a "scan" on the house to see if I could pick up anything else, and I sensed the presence of several adults and a little girl. None of them felt threatening, so we decided to leave the ghosts alone.

In September of 1988 the paranormal activity picked up. During a Girl Scout sleepover at our house the ghosts apparently decided to have some fun scaring the kids. They made noises on the stairs, in the walls and in the basement under the front living room where most of the girls were sleeping.

None of the girls slept very well and they couldn't wait to leave in the morning.

The next day five girls were still in the living room/office when I asked my oldest daughter where my keys were. She and I were standing about three feet apart. The keys lifted up off of a file cabinet where I had just looked, floated in the air a distance of five feet to a spot right between us at eye level, then dropped to the floor. All of the girl scouts saw this happen and ran - screaming—out of the house. They waited outside for their parents to pick them up. Of course, none of them would visit again. Now I knew I was dealing with at least one prankster spirit and did not appreciate it.

In January of 1989 I hired a new secretary (the first one quit due to paranormal activity while I was gone) and told her about the ghostly activity that had happened in the past but that it was pretty quiet now. She did not seem alarmed. I felt that I should tell her about it up front so she wouldn't be afraid if anything did happen. Not more than two weeks later I had to leave to do errands and came back to find my secretary wide-eyed and packing up her things. When I inquired as to why she was leaving she explained that she heard a noise in the basement and called out to see if it was my husband, Gene. When no one answered, she thought that he might be hurt and went downstairs to investigate. No one replied, but she did see a little girl (about age 11) with long blond hair in a white long nightgown standing by the furnace. When she asked if the little girl was ok, the girl slowly faded away and disappeared. I could not convince my secretary to stay after that incident.

I did another scan of the house and saw the little girl. She told me that she died in the house and it was because of the furnace. I did research but could find no reference to this incident. The only thing I could figure was that it may have been Carbon Monoxide poisoning due to a faulty heat exchanger or blocked flue.

I asked the neighbors in the area if they knew anything about the history of the house and found out that there were 11 people living in the house just prior to us. Since the room addition was incomplete, there was no heat or cooling in that part of the house so they must have all lived in the older, smaller side. That would have been very crowded. The neighbors reported that they heard a lot of fighting and yelling on several occasions, and that one or two of the men used to stomp up and down the stairs quite often. I also found out that a young girl was found dead in the house in the 1960's or 70's.

In the summer of 1990 the ghost became audible. I was cleaning up the kitchen while my daughter, M. and her friend Jennifer washed and dried the dishes. Our house had not yet been remodeled in the kitchen and the old original cabinets were still in place. The bottom drawer often stuck so I told my family to always leave it open slightly so we could get it open more easily. On this occasion, I went to the drawer and it was tightly closed, so I said, "Alright, who closed this drawer?" To which a man's deep voice replied, "I did." The girls and I looked at each other, dumbfounded. We questioned each other as to who made that remark, and we decided that I would ask the question again while we watched each other. I asked, and this time the ghost answered in a very annoyed manner. The reply was a louder male voice saying "I DID!" That was the last time that Jennifer visited us. I wish I had that on tape.

Not long after the kitchen episode, a ghost appeared in the window one evening. I drove up to the house after an outing with my daughters and as we pulled up to the side of the house a man pulled back the drapes and looked out of the window at us. We thought it was a burglar and went next door to call the police, who found nothing when they arrived. The doors and windows were all locked. My daughters and I stared at each other, knowing immediately that it was a manifestation of one of our spirits.

In 1991 I finally did a clearing of the house because one of the male spirits seemed to be gaining in strength and negativity. He did things to scare my daughters such as morphing posters of rock stars on the walls in my oldest daughter's room into hideous creatures. After my daughter complained of this, I watched one evening and witnessed it myself. I removed the poster and replaced it with another but the same thing happened. She also said she saw a dark figure floating around the room at night. I began to see evidence of something draining energy from both of my daughters because they seemed tired all the time and suspected that it was he. My daughters had not yet learned how to protect themselves fully against psychic attack and it was evident that something needed to be done.

I will not go into how the clearing was done here because it can be a very dangerous procedure if not done correctly and by an experienced psychic. Suffice it to say that the negative spirit is gone, along with the other adult ghosts in the house.

The little girl has since appeared to us several times. She starts out as a white mist, and then materializes fully except for her feet. She always wears a white long nightgown and floats in the air. The spirit can answer us by closing the basement door or knocking on it or something else in the basement. We feel her presence often. I have asked her if she would like to go to the light and get on with the next world, but as of 2006 she is not ready to go yet. It seems that she has a strong attachment to the house. Since she is doing no one any harm I will leave her alone for now.

The Portal

We have a portal located inside and outside the house on one exterior wall off of the deck. This portal appears at times in the shape of a round swirling hole and at other times as a four-pane window that I and my oldest daughter and other researchers can see. I was surprised to find that this type of portal appears to other people as well and has been photographed. We have not been able to get any photos of our portal yet. It used to open regularly in the fall each year and stay open for a few days or weeks at a time, but recently has been open all year-round.

During the time that this portal is open we may see spirits appear to go in and out of it. Often, these entities don't seem to notice me or anyone else and just pass through the portal and move through our yard to go on about their business somewhere. Sometimes, whatever comes to our world does seem to be observing me and/or my family. I am at a loss to explain why the portal is in that particular location, when it first appeared, or why it is there. Maybe it has always been there—even before the house was built. I have observed the portal on several occasions and it may be that this is how beings and spirits from other dimensions travel back and forth to this dimension.

September 1987: My husband and I were gone for a day and my two teenage daughters stayed behind. They had two girlfriends stay the night. My oldest child, Mia, saw a large face appear on the wall next to the staircase in the new addition of the house. She pointed it out to the other girls and they all saw it as well. The face was three-dimensional, and measured about 3' in height. It seemed to be looking at them. Mia said it appeared more alien than human but was not sure why it was there or what it was.

The face has not reappeared since, but a silvery mist has appeared in the same location several times. I suspect that whatever it was it came through the portal, which is approximately 20' from that spot.

October 2004: At a Halloween party in 2004 I asked a friend of mine, Chris Brethwaite, a paranormal investigator in the Kansas City area, if he could sense where a portal might be in the house. I told him nothing else. He found the spot within two minutes. Chris said he could feel a difference in the air and that it felt like a vacuum. He could not see it, but definitely knew where it was. I then asked another psychic friend of mine to come in the room and he located it in the exact same position. He also reported a vacuum like feeling when he placed his hand in the area.

October 2005: While my husband was out of town on his annual fishing trip with his dad I stayed home to run the business. On Sunday evening I took the trash out to the curb for the Monday morning pickup and when I returned to the deck on the side of the house there was a large black creature sitting in the middle of the deck. It had the head and upper body of a very large cat or small panther and the lower body and tail of a possum. I estimate that it was approximately 30" in length not counting the tail. I thought for a moment that this was an actual animal. It looked at me, then ran down the steps of the deck to the driveway and disappeared into thin air. I am sure this was a creature that entered from the portal.

September 23, 2006: I went out to the hot tub for my nightly spa (a necessity for people who work long hours) and almost immediately noticed a large eye, complete with detailed eyelid, pupil and iris at the portal area. It simply looked at me for a while then disappeared. I closed my eyes for a minute, then opened them again and saw a white rod shape about 6-8" in length over the sliding glass doors to the right of the portal area It stayed for one second, then darted into the wall over the doors. I got the distinct feeling that it was observing me. Obviously, the portal continues to open.

We have wood lattice work around our deck and I have noticed that while meditating I can see into another dimension by looking through the lattice. So far, I can only do this at night. I have seen other people and animals walking or moving about that seem oblivious to me. Sometimes I see eyes of different creatures looking in at me as if they are looking through a window. At times a whole face will be visible and sometimes they are not human. I have asked my guides what these creatures are and found out that they are 5th and 6th dimensional beings that share the same location as we do but because of their high vibration we do not normally see them. They are simply observing me when I observe them, but normally they do not watch what I or anyone else does. I catch a glimpse of these entities while in a meditative state, but not when I am going about my normal daily business. I have no reason to disbelieve them, but I am still cautious.

Aliens or Ghosts? August 29, 2006: My husband went out of town on an annual fishing trip and I was home alone. I should note here that most unusual events happen to me when he is not in the house. One evening, I was awakened at 3:00 AM to a loud, clicking sound coming from the doorway in my bedroom. It sounded like it was approximately 6' up from the floor. I was immediately wide awake and knew that something was not right. The sound was a series of six clicks that sounded like an animal noise. Each click had a different tone and style. I knew somehow that this was a communication from one type of creature to another, but don't know why I know that. I felt the presence of two beings in the room and looked around but saw nothing. We have a skylight above our bed and the moonlight was adequate to see everything.

A few minutes later I heard someone walking on our gravel driveway, and then the hot tub jets came on. Next, I heard a crash in the kitchen sink. Oddly, I fell back asleep when normally I would have turned on the light and gone downstairs to investigate something like that.

The next day I checked the sink and nothing was there. The cats were outside so they couldn't have made any of the sounds in the house. I called my daughters and found that they had experienced some very odd things the same night. My youngest daughter, R. had a baby prematurely and he was still in the hospital. She had to pump milk every four hours to take to him and was up at 12:00 am in her living room with the machine on when she heard a loud banging on the wall near the front door. (This is our rental house on Pearl) It was a methodical banging and she thought someone must be playing a joke on her. R. ran upstairs to see if either of her boys was kicking the wall. Both boys were fast asleep and not moving. The noise stopped when she left the chair, but she called her older sister anyway.

R.'s sister and her husband raced over to her house and walked the perimeter, then drove around the block and saw nothing. They headed back home, and then the banging started up again. This time, R. called the police and her sister, then Mia returned to R's house. Neither of them tried to call me but they wouldn't have been able to get me anyway because our phone was out due to a storm. The boys were still fast asleep. I did a reading on the house and could not determine the source of the banging noises—which is odd because I can usually pick up *something*.

Mia and her husband went home and went to sleep. She was awakened at 5:00 AM by a bright green light the size of a golf ball coming from the satellite receiver. Normally, the green light on the receiver is very tiny (1/4"), but it was very large and bright at this time, then it went back to normal size. Mia noticed that she was wide awake, and normally she would be very groggy at that time of the morning. *This is similar to my feeling of being wide awake when I heard the sounds at 3:00 AM.* Mia then noticed a bright, blinding white light coming underneath her bedroom door, but when she got up to open the door there was nothing there and the white light was gone.

Why all three strange events occurred on the same evening I do not know, but it seems too coincidental. In fact, it is extremely bizarre.

September 15 25, 2006: Our phone goes out whenever it storms. Somehow water gets in the line and after a few days it dries out and comes back on. This time, however, the phone did not come on for over two weeks so I called the phone company, who said they would come out the next day. That evening, while I was in the house alone the phone rang twice with the rings being close together. Only one phone rang—the others did not. At first I thought that SBC must have come out early and fixed the line, but when I picked up the phone it was still dead. The next day, the technician came out and fixed it and said they had not been out before. I don't know why or how that phone rang, but it was during a T.V. show I was watching on ghost hunters. Was it a message?

The next day the phone was out again. I called Birch to ask if they could do a line check and they said that the phone was off because I ordered a disconnection. I did not call them and neither did my husband. Now I am trying an internet phone service and we'll see what transpires with that!

October 12, 2006: My husband fell asleep on the couch at 9:30 and I got in the hot tub outside on our deck. I felt as if something was watching me but all was quiet. My dog, Gracie, then started to jump on the wood gate to her kennel, frantically trying to get out. I looked over in that direction and saw an 8' tall human-looking dark figure walk from one side of the shed to the other and through the wood fence into Gracie's pen. (I know the height because I was able to measure a point on the shed the next day where the top of the head was located.) The dog immediately stopped barking and trying to get out. I was concerned that something hurt her and tried to get my husband to go investigate, but he wouldn't wake up. So I locked the doors and went to bed, hoping that whatever it was would go away. I believe this creature probably came from the portal.

January, 2007: I got in the hot tub at around 10:30 pm and immediately felt like I was not alone, although everything was very quiet. There had been a recent snow and ice storm in the area, so it was quieter than usual. I then heard a clicking sound coming from a few feet behind me in the driveway, but since the deck has lattice and solid walls around it I couldn't see anything. There were a series of 10-11 clicks of different tones, similar to the clicking I heard in my bedroom several months before. It sounded like the noise was coming from approximately 6' off the ground. I felt that the sound was some sort of communication between two beings.

I practically froze with fear, which is unusual for me. I sensed danger, and immediately went in the house without looking in the drive. Normally, I would have stopped to look to see what it was, but I knew deep in my soul that the creature that made that noise was not anything of this world.

August, 2007: On August 18, 2007 I was sitting on the porch at around 10:00 p.m. when I noticed a flash of light in the sky just above the trees in our back yard. It looked similar to lightning, but was a very small, thin, white line that measured approximately 2" across if I held something up to cover it at arm's length. There were no storms in the area. Intrigued, I continued to watch the area for more lights, and sure enough, during the 20 minutes I stayed on the porch, I saw multiple flashes of tiny electrical charges of varying lengths and flash times. The longest flash time was a full two seconds. This seems to be longer than normal lightning. The flashes of light appeared around and up to approximately 15' over the trees but nowhere else.

On August 19, I returned to the porch in the late evening once again and noticed tiny white flashes of lights—this time over a tree not 20' from the house. It appeared that they were very close to me and not something far away. They also kept close to the tree, and did not appear anywhere else. I continue to observe this nightly.

January, 2008: I was sitting in the living room watching TV and glanced up to see an apparition of a tall man walk in front of the living room door and head towards the laundry room. I jumped up to grab my Nikon camera that was sitting on the dining room table nearby and took some photographs. The camera would not work at first (oddly) but after I took one picture of some flowers on the dining room table, I then took three more pictures in the direction of the laundry room. The camera was set to take three pictures in a row very quickly, so these were taken less than a second apart. The third photo (not shown) was completely whited out.

Photo number 1 with what appears to be a ghostly set of stairs that are not currently in the house.

The Ghost Hunter's Field Guide

Photo number 2 with what appears to be a distorted hand in front of the camera lens, as if to try to stop me from taking a picture.

January to September, 2010: A lot of paranormal activity is occurring in and around the house. The spirits present seem to be getting stronger, with the ability to touch us physically now. We believe that our increased attention towards communication with our deceased relatives is the cause of this recent activity, rather than spirits haunting the house. I have been devoting serious time to communication with my mother and other relatives while in my house. Following is a photograph taken during and after a communication session with five persons present. During this session, I went into a light trance state and telepathically communicated with several spirits, did automatic writing, and spoke with Nostradamus. My daughter saw a white mist go in the direction of the living room and followed it, then took a couple of pictures. See the following:

A white glowing ball of light is in the upper right corner of this photo. The white lights in the picture on the wall are reflections from the camera flash.

The Ghost Hunter's Field Guide

My Daughter's Haunted House

912 S Pope Street in Independence (now razed) was one of the most haunted locations I have experienced. The house was at least 100 years old at the time of our visit. My oldest daughter, Mia, rented this home in March of 1995 for a period of one year. She lived there with her husband and two small children. Mia was pregnant at the time and had her second child while living there in January of 1996.

Soon after moving in, Mia asked me to visit the house because she felt that it was haunted. She had already seen several apparitions and had poltergeist activity in the kitchen area. A black ghost cat roamed the bedroom, leaping from the dresser to the bed, and then running through the wall. There was a water leak that started suddenly and she could not get it turned off. She also saw the window in her room disappear and turn into a door. Several entities walked into the house from this location.

Right after my arrival to investigate in March of 1995 several dishes fell to the floor, even though no one was nearby. I felt the presence of several angry ghosts, so I went into trance to see who they were and what they wanted.

The first spirit was that of an older man named Peter who built the house. He felt much attached to it and felt that anyone living there was an intruder. I asked him if he knew that he was dead and he said yes but it did not matter, this was HIS house. Peter was the one making noises in the walls, turning water off and on in the bathroom and kitchen, and breaking dishes. I asked him if he was ready to leave and go to the light. He wanted to think about it and said he would talk to me if I came back later. I knew he was lying about wanting to talk to me again.

There were several other spirits at the location that are much older and have been there for hundreds of years—way before any houses were built in the area. They are Native Americans and are protecting the location.

I then turned my attention to something else that caught my eye while I was speaking to Peter. I saw several small "people" that looked more like alien grays. They moved back when they saw that I noticed them. It seemed as though they were very surprised that anyone could see them. I could sense that they were there to observe my daughter and when I asked about it they said yes, but it was none of my business, and to leave them alone because they had a job to do and they were not harming anyone.

After discussing this with my daughter, we used some techniques to protect her and her children. It worked, and she did not have any visits from the "aliens" or ghosts again. I drove past the location where the house was and still feel negative energy there. I think this may be a portal area where entities can come and go at will.

Crysler and Lexington Ghosts

There is a 100–year old+ house at the corner of Crysler and Lexington in Independence that was made into three apartments. There are two apartments on the lower level and one unit above them. This house is located on the exact spot where a civil war battle was fought near a railroad cut in 1864. I was called to investigate paranormal activity in both lower level apartments.

I started my first investigation of this property on the right side apartment of the building. The tenant, C.T. told me that she saw a dark shadow in the shape of a man move across the living room/dining room area on several occasions during the day and night. She reported that she also heard scratching and banging in the wall behind her bed and in her bedroom closet. Her two small children refused to go near the closet and she had to get out their toys and coats for them when they needed them. C.T. said that the activity increased in frequency since she moved in 12 months earlier and that it felt more menacing as time went by.

Immediately upon entering the apartment I could sense a heavy presence that seemed to move around the room. I went into a trance and saw a man wearing a long black trench coat, pants and boots that looked like 1860's attire standing in the dining room area. He had an angry look on his face and was looking right at C.T. The man said he did not want her or anyone else in this location because it belonged to him. He walked to the closet area. I could see that he didn't live in this house as it was, but lived at that location in a small cabin many years ago. The closet area was likely the original entrance to the log cabin and was where he walked in and out of this world. I did a clearing and afterwards, the spirit was quiet but he remained there.

I then visited the neighboring apartment to see C.C. who told me that she was experiencing banging noises in the wall adjacent to the right side apartment and heard loud footsteps in the vacant apartment above her. When she looked inside the upper level apartment there was no one there. She also saw her kitchen cabinet doors open and close on their own and saw a white shadow and a dark shadow on several occasions. C.C. said that the kitchen cabinets flew open and slammed closed, and dishes flew out of the cabinets and came crashing to the floor the night before my arrival, which is what finally prompted C.C. to call me.

After going into trance I saw the same man from the right side apartment passing through, and also a petite woman. The woman had no relation to the male entity and had died recently. She told me that she was trying to get C.C.'s attention because C.C. is psychic. She wanted help of some kind because she felt wronged. I was able to see what she needed help with, but we were unable to assist her.

I visited the apartment at a later date to do a clearing, which was unsuccessful. This happens when an entity is very strong-willed and thinks they have unresolved issues that must be taken care of before they move on. In this case, her spirit is unwilling to leave until things are resolved to their satisfaction.

Both tenants moved out after their 12-month lease was up due to ongoing paranormal activities at their apartments.

During a recent visit to the property I went in to a trance and saw several civil war encampments in the area with men in confederate uniforms. There were teepees of guns next to tents and burning fires with cooking utensils all around. I saw the men fire their guns, and noted that I could see flame come from the end of the guns when they were fired. The noise was deafening. I could see men on both sides get injured and fall. I saw injured men being carried away on stretchers and loaded into horse-drawn carts. They were headed to a nearby hospital, which was a large home that had been converted.

The soldiers fired across the railroad cut, which was unfinished at the time. There was intense and continuous fighting and many spirits still roam the area. It was extremely difficult to see the pain and suffering these men endured and I had to leave after a short time.

There is a place to stop next to this location on the West side of the corner where the marker is located. If you like, step out of the car and walk around the area and see if you can feel or see anything. I think this would be an excellent place to ghost hunt because of the extreme emotion that is left behind after a battle.

Mound Grove Cemetery Encounters

Some people would say we are nuts for visiting graveyards on Halloween Night and they may be right, but what better time to see ghosts that might be lingering? The reason we investigated this location was because of an incident that R.T. had several years earlier. She was 16 years old and had just had a fight with her boyfriend. R.T. decided to drive to the Mill Creek Cemetery to be alone and think. So for whatever reason, R.T. got out of her car and walked through the cemetery at—yes— midnight.

R. found a nice spot next to a tree and sat down. She was approximately 200 yards from the front gate. No one else was around (who would be?) and it was a very quiet, moonlit night. R. closed her eyes and meditated for a few minutes. The thought occurred to her that up to this point she had never actually seen a ghost, although people around her could and she felt somewhat jealous of them. She thought "What better time and place to see a ghost?" and said out loud "If there is such thing as ghosts, show yourself to me right now!"

Right on cue, a white apparition appeared over the hill. R.

couldn't believe it, but she stood up and stared at it to be sure. It moved towards her. Now she could see that this was the apparition of a woman wearing a long white nightgown. She had no feet and glided through the air. Panicked, R. started walking toward the car. The ghost followed. R. then started running, and glancing back she saw that the spirit moved faster towards her. Finally reaching the car, R. looked back and the ghost slowly faded away at the gate of the cemetery. It seems she could not go past the gate.

Location where the dark shadow of a man appeared, answered me, and walked towards us.

Spot where R.T. sat when she saw the floating lady. Note the gold streak across front of tombstone of a woman— could it be the ghost?

Our team of five decided to see if we could get the lady ghost to appear again so we could get her on film. We arrived at the cemetery at 11 pm and walked in through the front gate. We agreed to stay together at all times for safety. I started by filming the entrance and graves in the immediate area with my infra-red camera. Mia took the digital camera and took several shots because sometimes we get orbs or spirits on film that are not visible to the naked eye. This evening we saw a fog appear over some of the graves, and that is not visible on the film, but no apparitions made their appearance at that time.

We moved further into the park, and as we did so it got darker since we no longer had the streetlights illuminating the area. The moon was out so that helped a bit. As our eyes became accustomed to the dark we could see better. After a while, Donna and I decided to stay behind while Mia, Rachel, and Jamyi walked further on. For some reason, we forgot all about our agreement to stay together. Big mistake.

I looked around at some of the local gravestones and took notes. D. and I felt the presence of a couple of spirits but nothing materialized. I did some filming, and after what seemed like 45 minutes, I called out for M., R., and J. They did not answer. I walked a little ways down the road where it was very dark and called again. I heard Mia's voice answer me and saw what I thought was her dark, shadowy figure walking towards me on the small paved road. After a minute, the three women appeared at the top of the hill. I then realized that the black shadow walking towards me and that answered me was NOT Mia. I walked backwards away from it and told the three women to look at the bottom of the hill where they all saw the dark apparition of a man moving towards me. They froze and would not come forward. I moved quickly back up the other side of the hill from where I came, and when I looked back the figure was gone. The five of us decided we'd had enough that night and left pretty quickly.

Note: the cemetery now has gates and is locked at night, so I wouldn't suggest an after-dusk visit.

Ghosts or Men in Black?

This is truly one of the strangest reports I have ever received and I think you'll find it extremely odd, too. In late summer of 2003 I received a call from a woman who was much panicked. She is a housewife, and lives with her husband and two dogs. In her 63 years she had never seen anything like this.

Sara D. was awakened at approximately 5:30 a.m. on a Saturday morning by her dog, which needed to go outside. It was still dark outside and it was unusual for the dog to wake up that early. Sara got up and let the dog out the front door, then waited for him on the front stoop. She looked across the street and noticed that there was a newer black four-door sedan parked in front of her neighbor's house two doors down and across the street. She thought it was odd that the parking lights were on. Sarah noticed a male driver and possibly a male passenger in the front seat of the car, both wearing dark clothes. The passenger turned around and looked directly at her, and Sara could see that he was wearing sunglasses.

Sara then looked at the house, expecting a person to come out of the door to the waiting car. Instead, she saw a small, 6" - 10" diameter bright white light pass through the closed door of the house, then travel to the waiting car and enter through the back passenger side window. Immediately, Sara saw a third person sitting in the back seat who wasn't there before. The car took off quickly. Sara said she could swear that the light became a person when it went into the car. She thought that the quick retreat from the house was a reaction to her watching the car.

I went to the location the next day and scanned the area to see what I could pick up. I did not feel the presence of any spirits in the house or see anything unusual at the time of my visit. I did, however, sense that the people in the house Sara mentioned were being watched, but by whom (or what) I could not tell. The black sedan, men wearing black suits and black sunglasses certainly fit the description of "Men in Black." I do think that Sara is telling the truth about what she saw. She and her husband have since moved away to another state and oddly, their house burned down while it was vacant.

The Ghost Hunter's Field Guide

Dark Spirits Haunt Family

Another house on the East Lexington block is haunted by unfriendly spirits. The family told me of events dating as far back as 1976 when J.D. and his wife, Bettie, moved in the house with their two young boys, J.R. and A.

Not long after moving in, the entire family noticed that they felt like they were being watched all the time. None of them could explain it. While the husband and boys were away at work and school during the day, Bettie would notice this feeling more often. After a few months, Bettie noticed that things would get misplaced, only to turn up in an odd place. Keys would be missing from the key hooks by the door and turn up underneath a laundry pile. Her hair dryer disappeared one day, only to show up on the back porch a few days later. Her husband said that she must have moved these items and forgot about it but Bettie knew better.

In 1977, the youngest boy, A., age 10 started complaining that he was now afraid of the dark and would like a nightlight. This was odd since he had not been afraid of the dark before. He said he saw red eyes watching him at night. At first, the older brother, J., did not believe him but he soon started seeing the red eyes as well and also wanted the nightlight on. Soon that was not enough, and they started leaving on the table lamp. The boys started losing sleep because of the "monsters" in their room.

Their father still did not believe that anything unusual was going on and he did not experience anything unusual. Approximately two years after moving in the house, Bettie saw a Cheshire cat in the tree in their back yard. She thought it was her imagination at first and tried to ignore it. The cat looked like a cartoon cat with a big smile. It showed up on several occasions when she was alone, but would never appear when any one else was around. Bettie was afraid to hang her laundry outside anymore and asked her husband to purchase a dryer. He refused. She did not mention the cat for fear of sounding crazy.

As the years went by, more and more activity increased. Finally, all of the family members saw the red, glowing eyes and dark shadows in the upper bedroom that the boys shared. They all experienced hearing footsteps walk across the upper floor when everyone was downstairs. And everyone experienced missing items that would appear weeks or months later in odd places. An overwhelming feeling of negative energy in the house pushed the two boys to leave home early because they could not stand to be in the house. As soon as they each turned 18, they moved out. The parents opted to stay and hoped things would return to normal. They didn't.

Months would go by with no activity but as soon as anyone noticed that things were quiet around the house, something new would happen. It was as if someone or something was listening and reacting to the conversations of the homeowners.

Our paranormal research team was called to investigate the house in 1999. We arrived at the house, but none of us could go inside except Mia. We all felt an overwhelming heavy, dark, presence. I decided that we would do our investigation from another location and do remote viewing. Remote viewing is a term for observing things from far away, whether it is a city block or around the world. This is a technique that I used often in my investigations to find missing persons. While none of the rest of our team had used the technique before, they all quickly learned how to do it.

We split up and I asked each team member to see what they could find out on their own. When we compared notes it was surprising even to us how similar our findings were. Each of us saw a dark entity that could materialize at will. None of us felt it was human, but that it was similar to "Shadow People," such as those outlined in *The Secret War* by Heidi Hollis.

Shadow People are non-human entities that observe people and take energy from them. They can only live on fear generated by people, hence the menacing red eyes that would certainly scare anyone, especially a child. We all felt that the other paranormal activity in the house was generated by this dark presence that was growing in strength and also by several spirits of people who had passed on. I sensed that some of these were Native American spirits and they were angry about their land being disturbed.

I could only advise the family to leave the house as soon as possible as I had no experience getting rid of this type of Shadow entity. The house mysteriously burned down while the family was out of town in early 2006.

Note: I have observed two other Shadow People. The first happened in 1978. It was in the shape of a man who stepped out of some trees while my husband and I drove through a neighborhood. The man walked to the center of the road, then disappeared in front of our eyes. The second incident was in May of 2006. I saw a man wearing an old western-style coat and low wide-brimmed hat standing on the steps of the First Presbyterian Church on Lexington. He was all black from head to toe. The man stood there for a minute while I was stopped at a stop sign, then disappeared. I was quite shaken up by this incident and it still bothers me when I pass by this church. After recently visiting Mount Grove Cemetery where Joseph SmithIII is buried, I feel that his ghost does haunt the place occasionally due to some unfinished business.

Rotary Park Encounters

Rotary Park is located one block south of 23rd Street, and few blocks west of Sterling in Independence, MO. It is a popular place for children to play and for adults to walk on the track around the park. There is a creek on the South and West side of the park and a big hill on the West side beyond the creek.

My eldest daughter and I used to take walks in the park almost nightly starting in the spring of 2003. We did not notice anything unusual about it until September, 2003 when the park cleared out earlier in the evenings and was fairly quiet. Often, we were the only two people walking. One evening while briskly walking along on the East side of the track I felt a shaking in my entire body that started at my head and jaw, then traveled downward. The shaking stopped when I moved forward. I stepped backward a few steps and the shaking started again. I could feel a definite difference in the air in this one spot. My daughter stepped into the space and said she felt an "electrical" type feeling.

The next evening we returned to the park again. The spot was still there and felt the same to me. I was intrigued about it and

The Ghost Hunter's Field Guide

decided to go into trance to see what it may be. We sat on a park bench and suddenly I saw spirits all around the park. Some were Imprints, which are what I call *Imprints in Time* where a psychic can see events that happened in the past as if watching a movie. I saw small log cabins, several tent camps, lots of camp fires and many people milling about. A few of the apparitions were ghosts.

The first ghost is a man who hangs out around the South edge of the park. He looks like an old prospector and has a gold pan in his hand. He wears a dirty white shirt, suspenders, pants, boots and an old raggedy hat. I see a tent set up with a fire and pot in front of the tent facing the stream. The man means no one any harm, but he does not like it when people get too close to him. He seems not to realize that he is dead. There is an odd impression in the grass in this area where the grass blades move in the opposite direction of the wind at times. My daughter and I have noted this on several occasions. I believe that is where the man's tent was. The name he gave me is "Old George."

Another ghost is that of a young woman in her late 20's or early 30's. She wears a long dress and stands next to a large tree on the West center side of the park near the walking track. This is a good place to visit if you really want to feel a ghost. If you place your hand on the East side of the tree 12" away from the tree approximately 5' up from the ground it will feel noticeably colder or warmer than the air around it. We took a tour to this park on Halloween night in 2004 and all 11 people could feel the spot next to the tree. Three could see a white mist in the same space. I can see a woman materialize there and then turn to white mist. She told me her name was *Anne*. She feels much attached to the location. When I did a reading of the area, I got the name of Frank James but did not know why there was a relationship to this woman.

I asked a history buff friend of mine, Joe Rudzik, about this location and he told me that where there is currently a brick schoolhouse at the top of the hill is the exact spot where there was an older school. Frank James' girlfriend was the schoolteacher. In those days it was customary for a teacher to be unmarried. When the community refused to let the woman marry Frank James and still retain her position as teacher, the school mysteriously burned down.

Frank then offered to rebuild the school but only if his new wife could continue to teach there. The town council agreed, and the new school was built. I think this woman is the ghost of Frank James' wife. I did research on the internet and found that her name was *Anna* "Annie" Ralston (1853-1944). Frank James (1843-1915) is buried in Hill Park, directly North across 23rd Street and Anna is buried next to him. I believe her ghost haunts the park because she has a strong attachment to the school.

In October of 2007, I took a class outing to this park on two different nights. On both occasions everyone felt a difference in temperature next to the "Anne" tree and I was able to get several photos of orbs. One class attendee had is video camera battery suddenly go from 1 hour time left to 45 seconds in an instant. He was standing near the tree when it happened. Also at the same instant, I saw Anne come out of the tree. Perhaps she could not materialize until she had some energy from the battery.

Other spirits appear in the form of tiny bright orbs and flit about the tree tops. They occasionally wander down to the center of the trees. These feel like young children or possibly sprites (young, fairy-like creatures).

There are tree spirits in at least three locations in the park. Tree spirits are actual spirits of the trees and they have very individual personalities. They are visible to almost everyone who looks for them.

Old Ghosts and Strange Events

Fairmount is one of the oldest neighborhoods in Independence, Missouri. It is located off of 24 Highway. This area was a pioneer village prior to being divided up into Plats in 1860. This particular house was built in 1910 on top of a much older rock foundation and basement. The homeowner's dog digs in the yard and has retrieved old farm implements that look very old.

I was first called to investigate this house in 1987 and have returned many times since then. The activity continues to this day. The homeowners, F.K. and his wife A. have experienced spirits materializing on numerous occasions. I have seen one spirit of a man in a long old-west frock coat wearing two pistols. He has long hair and a beard. The man walks up and down the creaking stairs of the house, and can be heard at all times of the day and night. Since the current house was built after the time period of the clothing this ghost wears, I assume that there were steps in the prior house in the same location. This spirit means no harm, and seems unaware of anyone else. He is very serious about his work, and seems to be concentrating hard while he walks. I believe he was a deputy or marshal.

One night shortly after retiring for the evening, A. told. F. to look at their dresser. There, in full Confederate Civil War uniforms and swords were three tiny men standing on the dresser. None of the men were more than 24" high, but all were in perfect proportion. These three ghosts have appeared several times and they do react to the homeowner's when they notice them. A. and F. do not feel any malice from the spirits and do not want them to go. This is my first encounter with ghosts appearing in miniature and I honestly do not have an explanation for it. Obviously, the current house would not have existed during the civil war, but perhaps a camp or cabin was on the property prior to the building of this house.

In May of 2006, F.K. came into possession of his grandfather's white suit from the 1940's. He hung the suit on the outside of the closet and went to bed. A few minutes later, A. saw something in the suit and told F. to look at the suit because his grandfather was standing in it. A. had never seen F's Grandfather, so he asked her to describe him. She did and it was an exact description.

F. could not see his grandfather, but felt his presence, then felt someone lie next to him and put their arm around him. At first, F. thought it was his wife, but when he looked, she was too far away. He sensed that it was no one he knew, and this presence had nothing to do with his grandfather, but was a different spirit. F. slowly reached around, grabbed the hand and moved it off of him. F. says the hand was very pliable and felt something like jelly. He was too afraid to turn around to look at what it was. Luckily, he has not experienced the same thing since.

Trance work: I did a scan during a trance and saw a lot of activity over the years. There have been many people living on this spot almost continuously since the 1820's. I saw tents, then a cabin, then saw the cabin being torn down because it was not built very well. Later I saw a foundation being dug and a house built on top of it. That house burned down and was replaced by the current house. At one point, the property was seized (stolen) by someone who kicked out the previous rightful owners.

Historical research: F.K. did some research on at the Historical

Society and found that the area was a pioneer village in the early 1900's and later a favorite hangout of Frank James. A store James frequented was located only 2 blocks from this house. This area was a hubbub of activity, so it is no wonder that there are so many spirits here.

5/3/2007: The owners heard the sound of a music box coming from the upstairs bedroom. They do not have a music box. They also heard footsteps walking across the carpeting and stairs for several days in a row. The cat and dog acted strangely during the same time period—often following an unseen object around the room.

05/21/07: Three of the QUEST Team members re-visited the house at the request of the homeowner, who reported recent activity. The team stayed for over three hours, during which time the ghosts were very active. I first sensed something by the fireplace, where I then tested the area with the EMF meter. The meter spiked at the opening of the fireplace.

The three of us felt activity upstairs, so we all moved to the upper floor. As we walked up the steps, our team member Rachel felt a presence in front of her. I should note here that I have seen the spirit of a man on these steps on several occasions. Rachel used the EMF meter, and it spiked, and then stopped. As she moved forward, it spiked again. She was able to follow the spirit down the hall and into the far bedroom by using the meter. We had not experienced this before, but this was a very strong spirit. Upon entering the bedroom at the end of the hall, I saw it as it used to be approximately 100 years ago. There was a pot belly stove in the center of the back wall in front of an old chimney, floral wallpaper on the walls, a simple iron bed, and one dresser. Nothing fancy. The man who lived there was tall and wore a long coat and pistols. I believe this is possibly a deputy marshal or sheriff who rented the room from the owners. I sensed that he reported to work each day in downtown Independence.

Mia, our third team member, then opened the closet door and picked up psychically that someone was once restrained and kept in this room. There was an ominous feeling about it. We all wanted to leave the room immediately. I do not feel this was related to the (possible) Marshal.

Trance work: Next we moved to F. and A.'s bedroom. I had the sudden feeling that I should lie down on the bed and close my eyes, and did so. I fell into a half-trance and saw a single mother living in the house with an adult daughter. The daughter and mother were arguing over the daughter going somewhere by herself with no escort. There was no father in the house—I sensed that he was dead. The women both wore long flowered dresses with bustles that could have been 1870's-1890's attire. Why this was significant, I don't know yet.

We all moved into the hallway and as I glanced back into the bedroom I saw a column of whitish/green fog appear. I pointed it out to Maria and Rachel and the homeowner, who all saw it, too. It dissipated within a minute. We then looked down the hall to the far bedroom and saw fog again.

F. asked us to look in the bathroom where he saw faces in the carpeting but none of us saw anything there. We then moved downstairs, where a column of fog appeared next to the dining room table. I took a photo (see below) of where the fog appeared, which was to the right and in front of Maria. Maria was just starting to move, so the photo is blurry. But notice her arm—it appears to be transparent. This is exactly where I saw the fog. Note: no one else saw this particular fog except me; however, they did feel the presence of someone nearby.

May 31, 2007: F. reported that he was putting laundry away in his bedroom in the late afternoon when he heard the name "Zizzi" called out by his grandfather's voice. F. had been trying to contact his long-dead grandfather through meditation for some years with no success—until this occurred. He heard no other words. "Zizzi" means "aunt" in Italian, and is what his grandmother's family called her. F. is absolutely certain that it was his grandfather's voice.

June 1, 2007: F. reported to me that as he and his wife had just gone to bed when they both noticed a black, triangular shape object floating in the room. It appeared to be approximately 12" across and was shaped "kind of like the stealth bomber." The object darted about the room, hesitating over several areas, with most of the concentration being over them as they lay in bed. Then the object moved through a closet and into the chimney. The episode lasted approximately 10 minutes.

June 2, 2007: F. reported that a triangular shaped object appeared to them again, only this time it had a greenish glow about it and it stayed for a few minutes longer than the previous evening. This one also moved about the room, then darted through the closet and into the chimney. *Note: See the chapter in this book on haunted chimneys.*

October, 2007: A. told me that she sees ghostly nightgowns and heads of spirits floating in her bedroom at night. F. and A. both saw the full apparition of an old lady in old-fashioned (early 1800's clothing and bonnet) who turned to look at them, then faded away.

I decided it was time to find out exactly why there are so many spirits here and asked the couple to leave the house for an hour one evening. As I got comfortable on the couch a black, shapeless shadow moved across the ceiling of the entryway. I knew I was not alone at that point. I meditated and contacted several of the spirits who told me that there is a portal area near the chimney in the bedroom here and that most of them are ex-residents of other houses in the neighborhood.

They use this portal to move in and out of their dimension and sometimes congregate together there. That explains why we see so many non-resident ghosts at this location. They are simply using this spot as a gathering place and to use the portal travel to our dimension. The spirits are not "haunting" the occupants, they just happen to see them as they pass through.

The black shadow does have me a little concerned, though, as it felt rather ominous. Hopefully, it won't return.

July, 2010: The couple continues to have paranormal visitors, especially in the bedroom area. They have also had a number of sightings of what can only be described as tiny UFO's that measure approximately 10" - 12" in diameter. The descriptions are of airplane-like objects, rounded saucer-like objects, and triangular shaped objects both with and without lights. Some even appear to have tiny beings in the windows. Others seem to take photos with flashing lights around the room, and then disappear, always in the same location near the chimney.

The Ghost Hunter's Field Guide

Pearl House Haunting

This house, built in 1910, was converted to a zone C commercial property and beauty shop in 1970. We purchased it in 2000 and turned it into an office for our staff with the intention of eventually putting up a larger building and tearing down the old house. We moved in and almost immediately knew we were not alone.

The first incident occurred to my secretary. She was missing her scissors, tape dispenser, and stapler. We looked everywhere but could not find them. The next morning they were back in their proper spots. Next, we noticed lights would go off and on of their own accord. And finally, a white mist began to appear to my assistant, then to the rest of us. One day, while she was alone late in the office, my assistant, Tamie, said she saw an old lady walk by her desk and go into my office. The lady was transparent but clearly visible. I began to see the lady not long after. My night bookkeeper reported seeing someone walk through the front office and go into my office on a number of occasions. One evening she took a digital camera and took some photos of my office. In one photo, there is a white mist clearly visible.

We noted that every time we spoke of tearing down the building it angered the spirit and she would react by turning lights off or taking things and hiding them. I have still not retrieved many items and wonder where they are.

We did an investigation of the house and found out that the old woman used to live here by her self for many years and was attached to it. She did not want us to destroy it. During a trance, I also saw other activity from long ago with someone else who owned the property during the 1800's. I see a man wearing a long frock coat and hat who walks around the area surveying it—and I don't see any buildings at all in the area at the time he is looking at it. There are no lingering spirits from that time period, however.

We moved out of the building in 2005 and now use it as a warehouse. I drive by at night sometimes to find all of the lights on even though we know they were turned them off. Note: this house is next door to Pearl House #2 where a ghost likes to turn lights on as well. He might be visiting us at both places.

We have an alarm system and movement sensors on the building. In August of 2006 I was called by our alarm company, Barnhart Security, who said they had movement in the Southwest side of the building interior but no open doors or windows. I asked how that was possible and they said they had no explanation since the movement sensor is set at 40lbs. (it takes something at least 40lbs. to set it off). My husband and I rushed to the building and found that a ceiling tile had been moved out of place in the Southwest room. The tile was not like that earlier in the day and it is directly below some boxes and items in the attic that we cannot reach. Was the ghost telling us to look at these items? I won't know until we tear the house down.

Haunted Pearl House–Rental

This house is our rental property right next to the office. We purchased it in 2003 to use as a showroom, and then turned it into a rental. The first family who rented it stayed for the contract period but left after a year due to ongoing paranormal activity. I saw a man on the roof one evening and thought it was a prankster until he disappeared right in front of my eyes. On at least six other occasions I saw a man looking out of the dining room window, but no one was in the house when we investigated. Other people saw someone looking out of the windows in our direction, too. Lights seemed to go on at night of their own accord, and we all heard footsteps on the basement stairs.

I decided to do an investigation and called the team out one evening. Three of us went into trance and got similar information. During our session we all heard loud footsteps on the basement stairs, but when we went to look there was no one in the area. We searched the whole house but found nothing. We did pick up some muffled voices on the digital audio recorder.

All three of us got information that there was an older man by the name of George who lived in the house alone for many years after his wife died. He got into a routine and did the same thing every day—cooking, getting dressed, reading, turning lights on, etc. He did not like the dark. The man was retired from the military and lived on a fixed income. I did not see a vehicle, so I think he was homebound.

I called my friends at Barnhart Security and told them of the strange events going on. They installed an alarm system for us and then set up an elaborate movement activated camera monitoring system that was hooked up to a computer. The system was in place for two weeks, then the installer took it away to review it.

The technician called me and said they were surprised to find something on tape. The T.V. camera was tripped on at 1:00 AM, and then the light in the living room came on of its own accord. You could see the switch move up on the video. Now everyone was very excited about this as it proved that something was going on. This was Barnhart's first ghost on tape, and even though no apparition showed up we all felt it was significant and proved that there was an entity in the house. Now Barnhart offers ghost hunting surveillance services.

Subsequently, we have had several QUEST meetings at this house because it is a convenient location for all of us. We have done trance and medium work to work on missing person and homicide cases, and have had good results contacting people who have passed on while working at this location. Additionally, during each of our sessions it never fails that some type of paranormal activity will occur. I suspected that there is a ley line or energy vortex at this location, and did dowsing with my L-rods. The rods, say yes, this is a vortex, and ley lines intersect here. So it is no wonder we have good luck contacting spirits at this location.

Hint: The concept of ley lines were proposed by Alfred Watkins in 1921 in his books Early British Trackways *and* The Old Straight Track. *Watkins believed that the ancient civilizations created straight line paths between monuments, although he attributed no supernatural quality to them. Now ley lines are considered to be locations of psychic energy. Where two ley lines intersect, or when one ley line has several important monuments, the energy is more powerful.*

Old Independence Library Building and the Lady in Red

228 & 230 W Maple Avenue, Independence, Missouri

This old building on the Independence Square at Osage and Maple is where two of our stores were once located. We moved in during September of 2005 and worked on the stores until January and February until they were opened. We stayed there for three years. The location also housed our offices and our paranormal investigative team met there often to discuss cases. Everyone who spent any amount of time here quickly found out that the place is very haunted. I will relate a few of the events that occurred.

I found out early on that this structure was built possibly around 1880 and used to be the old Independence Library where Bess Truman worked, and where Harry picked her up every day for lunch before they were married. Harry worked at Clinton's Soda Fountain, which is only two blocks away. The building has also housed a number of businesses in the past including Montgomery Wards and a jewelry store. It has now been divided in to several shops but the exterior remains the same.

During the period that we worked on the stores to get them ready we did some extensive remodeling. On a number of occasions we had electric power tools stop working even though there was no breaker thrown, and then start again. We wondered if a spirit was playing tricks on us. We heard voices on several occasions but when I investigated the source could not find anyone there. The voices continue to this day, often fooling my assistant, our bookkeeper, and Victoria's store manager or one of our clerks into thinking that one of them said something. The voices are usually unintelligible, but on some instances can be clearly heard. Often a disembodied voice will answer a question in a clear "yes" or "no" answer.

Lady in Red: We had a camera set up with a monitor in the back office so we can see when someone enters the store. On several occasions I have seen a woman dressed in red with white trim on her collar and red hat in what appears to be 1920's or 1930's clothing appear on the monitor. She has short, dark bobbed hair and carries books in her left arm. The lady walked determinedly through the middle of the stores, then through the center of the fireplace store through heavy cast iron stoves we had on display, then through the wall on the East side through a mantel. I believe that wall was an addition to the original building so it may be that it was not there before she died. It seems at times as if she is floating rather than walking, and at other times to walk normally.

Sometimes a spirit will open and close the front doors on each of the stores. The bell goes off and the doors open, but there is no one there. These doors are very heavy solid wood and could not possibly open due to wind or any other reason. We (I and my employees) have seen some apparitions that look like solid people appear then disappear. This phenomenon occurs almost on a daily basis. There were several days when we saw someone walk in the store, but when we go to assist them there isn't anyone there. I believe this phenomenon is a *Time Imprint,* rather than a haunting. It can occur in places where lots of activity took place over a long period of time, which would certainly be the case here.

October, 2006: We continue to experience spirits on a daily basis. They are especially active during October and November when the veil between the two worlds is thinnest. Sometimes it can get very annoying when you are trying to get your work done and get interrupted by the door bell, go out to greet a customer, and there is no one there - or you hear a person moving around and no one is around the area.

I taught a class on ghost hunting at this location in late October and during the class a couple of the attendees noticed someone walking behind the curtain that leads to my office. No one was in there and there is no other way out. They were quite excited to have seen a ghost appear during the class.

After the class, I was talking to Chris Brethwaite, a friend of mine who is a paranormal researcher. Chris was drawn to an area in front of a mantel display where he saw a woman appear. I did not see her, but felt a presence and saw a white mist. I walked to the area and we both noticed a very cold spot at that location. I took an EMF reading, and the meter spiked in that area. The spot warmed up after about 2 minutes.

December, 2006: A heavy Sony camera and case flew off of one of our bookshelves while we had a lot of customers in both stores. I heard rustling of papers before it happened but was too busy to investigate. I got the feeling that the spirit was upset that we weren't paying attention to it. I asked it to quit the pranks and they stopped for a few days.

January, 2007: My assistant and I were talking over lunch one day and I told her about how my deceased grandfather, Boyd Kithcart, recently contacted me while I was trying to communicate with my other grandfather, Frank Lombardo. Right as I explained how he contacted me we both heard a violent shaking of metal objects next to the window in the office. I looked around the area and found no metal except for a heavy file cabinet. I don't know how that sound was made, but we both figured that Boyd was just letting us know that he is alive (in spirit) and well.

June 4, 2007: I was watching the monitor when I saw a man's head appear in the store, then turn and go through a wall. The head was completely black. This is something new.

July, 2007: We had another alarm go off at the store –
This is the fourth time it has been set off for no apparent reason. The alarm company said movement is setting it off, but we can find nothing in the stores that could move- except for ghosts. Two police officers met me at the store to examine the area. I finally told them after talking with them for 15 minutes that the only answer must be ghostly activity, and to my surprise, they were not surprised at all. The officers told me that they get frequent paranormal calls in Independence. Now, I know there is a lot of haunting going on in this town, but for it to be so widespread that the police think nothing of it is amazing.

October, 2007: I taught the "Haunted Independence" class here one evening and we had three incidents. Several people told me they saw the heavy curtains I have in a doorway move on their own. These are too heavy to move due to air currents from the air conditioning. It is the same location where someone saw an apparition during class last year. I saw the floating head of a man appear in front of one wall, and another woman saw it, too. She described it exactly as I saw it—with dark circles around his eyes and very creepy looking.

Next, a woman in the class said she saw a lady wearing a white lace dress that was calf-length and black patent leather shoes. The lady kept saying "look at me—I'm very fashionable." She has blond hair. This is the exact same description that Chris Brethwaite gave me the previous year of a ghost that appeared to him in the same location. We felt her presence at the front of the store.

This is an example of how spirits may appear when you talk about them, and this phenomenon is fairly common. I guess it would be curiosity on their part—or maybe they are just letting us know that "yes, we are here."

Haunted Chimneys

Are chimneys portals to other dimensions? Do spirits enter and return through these portals? Since my contracting company does chimney inspections and repair, we are around fireplaces and chimneys constantly. We have noticed a pattern of ghostly activity and orbs around chimneys, and I am beginning to think that this sort of activity is fairly common. I also have a theory as to why paranormal events happen around chimneys, but more about that later.

I have thousands of pictures of chimneys and fireplaces taken with digital cameras. We started noticing that orbs were showing up in some pictures when a very dramatic photo with colored orbs showed up in May of 2003 (see chapter 7– Photographing Ghosts). This was the first time I noticed anything unusual in the photos, and it prompted me to watch for other anomalies around chimneys when inspection reports come in. We started using digital cameras in 1999, before that we used 35 mm film which never showed anything out of the ordinary.

Digital cameras pick up more of the Ultra Violet spectrum, so they sometimes get things that the naked eye can't see. In all but one case, the inspector did not see anything at the time, but the strange items appeared when the disk was put in the computer.

In the past several years we have collected quite a few photos that show something unusual in them such as colored orbs, white orbs, white streams of heavy fog, and in one instance—a clearly defined face of a man in the back fireplace wall. In every case, I compared the rest of the photographs taken at the same time and of the same chimney, and in all but one instance they show nothing unusual. It is usually *one* photograph that catches something, and the rest of the photos at the same location don't show anything. There is only one chimney so far where an orb appeared three different photos from different angles, and in the case of the face in the fireplace, it can still be seen with the naked eye at the home.

We do approximately five inspections per day with 6-12 photos taken at each house, so the photos with anomalies are only a small fraction of the total number of photos we have on file. In my opinion, that means that it is probably pretty rare to catch an orb or ghost on film.

Ghostly Encounters around Chimneys

In 1989 our company swept 350 chimneys at Fort Leavenworth, Kansas. We ran into three ghosts at Leavenworth that were rather uncooperative and apparently did not appreciate us disturbing them. The fort was established in 1827, and has a long history of spirits. At least nine ghosts have been officially reported, but there are likely more that have not been reported. During our work, several highly unusual events occurred that can only be attributed to the paranormal. Unfortunately, we do not have photos of any fireplaces since photography is not allowed on the base. All of the chimneys are constructed with bricks and mortar.

House #1: This house is the oldest building on the post and was originally a chapel. The chapel burned down in approximately 1827, and a clergyman named Father Fred was killed in the fire. A new house was built on the same spot in the 1830's— presumably using the same chimney. While we were sweeping the chimney, coal dust started coming through the entire masonry wall in the living room. There were no holes or cracks in the masonry! The entire lower level of the house was dusted with fine, grey coal soot and we had to go back and spend 8 hours vacuuming and cleaning up. What a mess! I was mortified, since nothing like that had ever happened to us.

The colonel's wife was not upset at all, and calmly explained to me that the problem must have been caused by their resident ghost! She told me that right after moving in to the house, they hosted a party for the officers and their wives. During the party, a woman screamed when she saw a face of a man in the fire in the fireplace.

Everyone in attendance saw the same thing and ran screaming out of the house. Evidently, it was quite a scene. After that, the family saw the apparition of a man floating on the landing next to the chimney on several occasions. He was wearing a clergy outfit, but his feet did not materialize when he appeared. He also appeared on many occasions in the fire, so the family quit using the fireplace. Well, at least it is clean now. I hope that ghost appreciates it.

House #2: Built in the later 1800's, this is a large three-story home. The occupant (the wife of an officer) notified us upon arrival that the room we were going to be working in was haunted, and the ghost often closed the door. She noted that she was leaving the door open all the way and that the door was off balance leaning in towards the room, then she left us to our work. I tarped off the fireplace, then sent a tech up to the top of the chimney to start sweeping. While standing alone in the room, the door suddenly slammed shut. I quickly ran over to the door and opened it to see if anyone was around, but there was no one in the hall. I then heard strange noises and talking coming from the fireplace and called the sweep on the radio to see what was going on. She said she did not say anything, and of course there was no one else on the chimney with her. When the lady of the house returned, she was not surprised to hear about the goings-on. She also told me that it was common knowledge among the residents at Fort Leavenworth that there is a lot of ghostly activity going on in the older houses. We packed up our gear and got out as quickly as we could.

House #3: Built around 1840, this is a two-story brick house with slate roof and brick chimney. I was outside by the van talking to the homeowner. One tech was inside at the fireplace, and another tech was outside on top of the roof doing the sweeping. Suddenly the 40' ladder fell over on its side—seemingly pushed by someone who wasn't there. The occupant and I both saw it fall over. The sweep walked over to the place where the ladder was but could not get down until we got the ladder back up again. This was a 40' heavy aluminum ladder that weighs 80 lbs! There was no wind that day *and* it was tied down to the gutter with a bungee cord! I had to call in another crew to get the ladder back up so the sweep could get down. The occupant of the home told me that they have a mischievous ghost who lives with them and causes havoc frequently. He said that the ghost hung around the fireplace most of the time.

    I did an internet search to see if there was any more information about Fort Leavenworth, and it turns out there are several books written about the subject that you can buy at the museum on the post, and other information on websites. From *hauntedhouses.com* I found the following information regarding the fireplace at 605 McClellan, located in the McClellan Officer's quarters. This house is a large three-story home. Apparently when a family moved in this house in 1975, a spirit made itself known to them. While enjoying a warm fire in the fireplace, the family was "gripped with fearful fascination" when an apparition of a man with a mustache and goatee appeared in the middle of the flame. When the fire died out, the face of this ghostly man appeared and remained on the back of the fireplace. This case sounds like the face in the fireplace I mentioned earlier.

Recently a program on ghosts was presented on the Discovery Channel. The occupants of the house said that every psychic investigator that has gone through the home notices that one of the entities comes in through the flue and stands in front of the fireplace. The temperature where the ghost stands is noticeably colder than the surrounding area. Other TV programs and internet articles mention ghosts around chimneys.

Why chimneys attract spirits

    In doing research on ghosts in the Kansas City area I talked with several other ghost hunters including Chris Brethwaite, a local Kansas City paranormal investigator and author. Chris and others have mentioned to me that they have noticed more paranormal activity around rivers, streams, and railroad tracks. I realized that in our ghost hunts that was true. A graveyard next to a river is more active than one that isn't. I got to thinking about what those features have in common with chimneys. It is *movement*. There is a flow of energy in any river, stream, or railroad track. And the correlation with chimneys is *draft*, the only difference being that chimneys are vertical rather than horizontal.

All chimneys are designed to create draft to remove toxic flue gasses and smoke from the fireplace or appliance without mechanical means. It is simple physics that makes a chimney work. The temperature differential between the outside of the chimney and the inside of the house is basically what creates draft. Draft is different at certain times of the year, being stronger in the cold winter months, which is also the time of year that people spend more time around the fireplace and fire up their gas furnace.

However, draft in a chimney occurs all of the time, even when it reverses because something is wrong with the system or house. The pictures we have taken of ghosts and orbs are from all seasons of the year.

I have found in my own investigations and have heard from other ghost hunters that spirits often appear in or around fireplaces and chimneys.

My theory is that the draft created by the chimney creates a doorway or portal between dimensions.

Two faces appeared in this fireplace on the back and right side walls immediately after the brick face and mantel were removed, but no face was there before the renovations. They remain there to this day, no matter how much wood is burned or how much soot is created. Both the homeowner and the chimney contractor were baffled by this.

Diagram of a typical masonry chimney

I suspect that ghosts use chimneys to travel to and from the spirit world and they do so through draft.

Draft can reverse when something is not working right or if the house is under negative pressure.

Draft going up a chimney

The picture above was taken by a chimney inspector during a routine visit. The inspector did not see the stream of ghostly fog going from the window area upwards, but it showed up on this photo when printed.

Courtesy of HearthMasters, Inc.

The Ghost Hunter's Field Guide

This photo was taken by a chimney inspector on a clear day. Most paranormal investigators agree that the colored orbs are rare. Note the half orbs at the bottom of the photo. See the color photo on the back of this book.
Courtesy of HearthMasters, Inc.

The Most Haunted House in Missouri?

Note: Do not try to visit—this is a private residence

I could write an entire book on this extremely haunted house. My family moved into this large 1850's home on Calhoun Street in Springfield, Missouri near Drury College in 1972. The first time I walked over the threshold I passed through a cold spot and said to my mother "This place is haunted." I was 14 at the time. She felt the cold spot, too, and agreed with me.

The night we moved in this Civil-war era home we had all just gone to bed when we heard my sister, who had a room at the end of the hall, scream. My father and 9-year old brother and I ran to find out what was wrong. I looked at the bed and spoke to her. In the dark you could see someone in the bed with the covers on, and we thought it was my sister. However, her voice came from the closet where my sister was hiding and she said there was a ghost in her bed. I turned the light on and as I did so, we all saw a ghost of a man in the bed who promptly disappeared -and we watched the covers slowly fall down. After that my sister moved her bed into the large closet. The ghostly visits were a daily occurrence.

Not long after settling in the house I noticed something odd about the walls. I could see small 3" -5" size three-dimensional faces of people in the walls. The faces moved around and talked, but I could hear no sound. At first, I was a little frightened but saw that they were oblivious to me, and I was just watching scenes from the past (time imprints). There were so many different faces that I wondered where these people could possibly have come from. We decided to investigate the past history of the place and found out that a doctor used the house as a hospital. That was the reason for the elevator in the house, and it would explain the presence of spirits and the number of faces in the walls. In later years, my mother admitted to seeing the faces, too, but she didn't tell me at the time because she didn't want me to be afraid.

We often heard footsteps walking on the wood floors and the cat would follow invisible things around the rooms. Sometimes the cat would jump in our laps as if she were afraid of something unseen.

One day, I was home alone doing ironing and listening to James Brown on the radio when an announcement came on that a man just escaped from the local jail. A few minutes later I heard loud footsteps on the stairs and second floor. I thought my father had come home and entered through the back door as usual, and then went upstairs. However, when I looked out the back door his car was not there.

I had no way to contact my mother so I called the police, who thoroughly checked out the entire house. They asked me if I knew there was a shotgun on my parent's bed, and I said I had no idea if my dad had it out or not, but that he did own a gun. The police left and I locked up the house. Later, when my family returned I found out that no one had taken the shotgun out of the locked cabinet. They caught the jail inmate shortly later on the other side of town. So apparently, this ghost could not only make loud stomping noises, but also had the ability to get a gun out of a locked gun safe!

Sometime during the summer I had a chilling event happen at around 9:30 pm. I had just gone to bed when I noticed a very white/blue light shine through my window. It was so bright it almost blinded me. I could not locate the source of the light, but something caught my attention in the vanity mirror across the room. I clearly saw a woman dressed in a black high-necked old-fashioned 1900's dress with a wide-brimmed hat. She was stabbing a younger woman with a large knife. The other woman was wearing a white high-collar dress. The young woman was screaming, but I could hear nothing. I was apparently looking at a reflection of something in the mirror that happened at this location sometime in the past.

To add to the drama, the large Victorian mansion just two doors down from us has its own story, which may or may not be related to the goings on at this house. We looked up newspaper archives and found out that a famous dentist lived and worked in the mansion in the late 1900's. He was obsessed with teeth, and kept all that he pulled. Apparently, this doctor went insane and when Mayor's wife visited him to have one tooth pulled, she woke up to find ALL of her teeth gone!

This incident so enraged the Mayor that the dentist knew he was headed for jail, so instead he took his own life by hanging himself in the house. The story leaked to the press and apparently the dentist's son could not take the bad attention and killed himself in the same manner. I wonder if the energy in this area is so bad that it affects the houses around it, including the one I lived in.

In 2004 while in Springfield for a convention, my friend Donna and I stopped by the house. I wanted to see if it was still haunted after over 30 years, and she agreed to accompany me to the front door. My intention was to talk to the current owner, but I noticed that there were no shades on the windows and no furniture. The only thing in the house were a few books were strewn on the floor. It looked vacant, but I rang the doorbell anyway.

The house is arranged so that you can see inside the window of the front door, through the window of the foyer door, and out through the window of the back door. The sun was shining through the back door and illuminated everything inside. Donna and I were about to leave when I decided to try the bell again. She and I both saw an old woman with white hair dressed in a long black dress walk slowly around the corner in front of the back door. She was using a cane. Then the woman disappeared before our eyes. Donna immediately turned and left saying *"Looks like it's still haunted and I'm not hanging around for more!"*

The bedroom where the bright light and vision of a murder appeared

The 1859 Jail

217 N Main Street, Independence, MO

In January of 2006 my In-laws visited my husband and I, and we toured the 1859 Jail, Marshal's home and Museum run by the Jackson County Historical Society. The jail has seen a lot of inmates and other people come and go, including women and children during the pre-civil war hostilities as well as during the war and later. One of the more famous "guests" that stayed here was Frank James.

It was our first visit to this building. Immediately upon entering the inmate area I felt the presence of several spirits. This did not surprise me at all considering the age and history of the building, but I was taken somewhat aback by the heaviness of the air. I knew that all of the spirits were not benign. As we walked past the 12 cold limestone cells, I could feel the loneliness and despair of the inmates from long ago. I could have looked at the past to see what happened then, but tried to shake off that feeling and see what I could tell about any lingering spirits instead.

I could see several people inside one tiny cell because there was no room for all of the inmates. Some of the people had done nothing wrong and felt greatly wronged by their accusers. I heard crying that sounded like children or young women, and saw a pregnant woman. Later I found out that women and children who were "on the wrong side" were kept in the jail just before and during the Civil War.

Upon entering Frank James' cell I immediately felt his presence and personality. Knowing nothing of Frank prior to this visit, I was surprised to find that he was intelligent, could read and write quite well, and was obviously well-educated and well-mannered. Surprisingly, I did not sense that he was really a bad guy, or that he thought he was bad at all, which was not exactly what I was expecting from an outlaw. When we toured the museum later I found that my assessment of Frank was exactly right, and that he was friends with the governor of Missouri and other high officials.

While still in Frank's cell I picked up another, more sinister spirit. This was a lingering ghost who stays behind and lives in that cell or near it. The spirit is a tall heavy-set Caucasian man with dark long hair that he pulls back. He also wears a long beard. He feels that he is trapped in this location forever and he is somewhat insane. I believe that he takes energy from people who visit, and that keeps his spirit going. I would not attempt to confront him as he is extremely negative.

I then saw a tall African-American man incarcerated here who has a strong personality, was a murderer, and was afraid of no one in his lifetime. I also saw a fight between two prisoners who were in cells across from each other. Interestingly, a lady and her daughter came into my shop recently and related a story about how during their visit to the jail someone grabbed the daughter's arm and when she looked around there was no one there. Then she saw two men in Civil war uniforms (one Union, one Confederate) fighting and shaking their fists at each other through the cell bars. One man was released from his cell and the guard handed him his guns. The man then turned and shot and killed the man he was arguing with right in front of the guard. The woman was so frightened by this sight that she will not return for another visit.

We toured the Marshal's home and when we got to the large bedroom area upstairs I could feel the presence of a strong woman. She does not want to leave and is very attached to the home. She feels that it is her home and all the visitors that go through there now are intruders. The woman does walk around to other parts of the building, including the gift shop area, and lets people know she is there. I hear the name of Cassie.

Note: every year during October, the Independence Square Association hosts ghost tours, and the jail is one of the stops. Go to www.theindependencesquare.com for more information.

Thurnham Hall, Lancaster, England

My husband and I made a trip to the Lake District in England in April of 2005 and stayed in a wonderful 12th century Jacobean stone manor house called *Thurnham Hall*. Immediately upon entering the hall I felt the presence of several spirits. One was a short, very stocky man with red hair who was trying to get his big leather lace-up boots off. I had visions of straw on the floor and animals inside the building. The man took off a sword that looked too big for him to carry. I asked where he was from and he said in a heavy accent "Scotland, of course." He came here on an invitation from the king and was helping to fight and protect the lands. This was a very early time period— the 1100's— and he was still very attached to the place. The ghost often pulled tricks on guests because he felt that he still had some ownership of the place, but he was very much aware that he was dead.

The second spirit was that of an older woman whose domain

was the kitchen and lower level. She told me she was the head of the household and was in charge of the manor. I saw a little boy near her who was very attached to her. This child's parents were not around much and the older woman took care of him most of the time.

On the third evening of our stay, the activities director took the guests on a tour of the building and told stories of the ghosts that choose to occupy several rooms in the large hall. I couldn't wait to hear what he had to say, since I already knew this place had several spirits. He told us of several reports by guests of children in old-fashioned clothing playing on the grounds, and a ghostly woman who picks up twigs on the lawn.

Our guide then showed a VCR tape of a room that had been occupied by a man who killed his wife in the 1700's. The tape had been made by a film crew from British television who brought along a psychic to do research for a program on ghosts. I filmed the TV screen as the guide played the tape for us.

Everyone in the room gasped as hundreds of tiny white glowing orbs appeared. The orbs came to the top of the fireplace opening, hesitated a second, then quickly exited the fireplace into the room. Most shot across the room and through the walls in several different directions. This continued for at least two full minutes. I checked the chimney for draft after everyone left the room and it was drafting strongly UP, so any theory about dust particles mistaken for orbs coming DOWN the chimney can be ruled out.

Next, the tour guide took us to the library where we all sat around in chairs while he and his wife stood on the balcony and explained that Jane Seymore lived in the hall before her (unfortunate) betrothal to King Henry the Eighth. The guide also said that the ghost of an old woman had been spotted in the library and the chapel next to it. Just before he started talking about the ghost, I saw an apparition of an elderly lady wearing floor-length skirts walk right through the guide's wife and head towards the chairs on the balcony. No one else in the room saw this, so I kept quiet, all the while thinking that the current tenants really have no idea how haunted Thurnam Hall is.

Ghost Trains

I saw my first ghost train in 1993 near Wichita, Kansas. My two daughters and I were heading home from a trip when Mia said she saw a man riding on a horse, then a train. The three of us noticed smoke to the left of the highway. We watched in amazement as an old-fashioned big black steel steam locomotive chugged along, then disappeared into an embankment. We stopped the car to check the area and sure enough, there is a set of railroad tracks that must have been there for some time. They lead directly into the embankment, which must be something that was added later. The train was apparently following its old schedule when we happened to pass by.

We've seen ghost trains in Independence, too. Since our move to Independence in 1987 I noticed a problem with a railroad crossing near my home. It seems to go off of its own accord, even when there is no train in sight. Sometimes the bell continues ringing for a long time, and I have called the railroad on a number of occasions to complain. However, it may not be the fault of the railroad.

While approaching the intersection at Scott and 20th Street one day at approximately 8:00 A.M. I noticed that the red crossing lights were on. I looked down the tracks to the East and saw a train with a small puff of smoke billowing out and its big bright front light on. It appeared to be about a quarter-mile away and moving very slowly. After crossing the track, I looked back but no train was in sight! I realized then that the problems with the crossing probably had nothing to do with the current railroad trains.

This railroad cut and set of tracks dates to the Civil War era, and is the same track that goes by the Lexington house mentioned earlier in this book. I've also noticed a transparent train at the old Independence Depot on a couple of occasions while crossing the bridge on Lexington. The train looks perfectly intact, and is complete with smoke billowing out the top, but you can see through it. The depot is very near the Lexington street location mentioned earlier in this book. I wonder if it is the same train traveling by my house at the Scott intersection. It might be worth a trip to the depot to see if you can see the ghost train.

The Ghost Hunter's Field Guide

1880's Victorian Ghosts

Photo taken of the home prior to 1920-Courtesy of Kent Dicus

The house today

The Ghost Hunter's Field Guide

In November of 2007 I did an investigation of an 1880 Victorian mansion in Garfield Heights in Northeast Kansas City, Missouri with the assistance of Chris Brethwaite and Frank K. The homeowner, Kent Dicus, reported that he and his friend Michael experienced some unexplainable activity in the home. We took along all of our ghost-hunting equipment for a night-time investigation. Oddly, my digital voice recorder was missing from my bag when I arrived even though I know I put it in just before leaving my house. Thankfully, Chris had his with him. When I returned home that night, the recorder was back in my bag.

When we arrived at the home, I immediately felt a presence of a man in the foyer; however, we proceeded to the kitchen to get our gear ready. We started in the basement, and I felt a heavy, dark feeling. One room in particular had the feeling of death in it, and I picked up a young boy living in that space and having breathing problems. The room was cold, damp and moldy. As we all moved towards the stairs to go back up to the kitchen, we noticed that the string for one of the lights was rotating in a circular fashion like a pendulum even though no one had touched it. It kept going for several minutes, much longer than one would expect.

I was surprised to get results in the first room we went into on the first floor. I heard the word "library" several times and Kent confirmed that that room was indeed originally the library as he had found that word written on the wall behind the fireplace mantel. The EMF meter spiked almost everywhere in the room including areas not around any electrical wiring, and the digital recorder picked up some muffled sounds here.

Next, we moved to the foyer, where I sensed the presence of the original owner of the house. He spoke to me telepathically and said that he designed and built the house and was very proud of it. He was pleased that the current owners took so much care to restore it to its original condition and use. Over the years it had been used for other purposes, including a home for unwed mothers and later for the elderly. Kent confirmed that the first owner was indeed the designer of the house. The spirit wanted me to go upstairs.

The owners led us to the second floor. The guest room had photographs of ancestors on the mantel. I felt the presence of some particular people that are watching over Kent, and he indicated that he felt that was correct. Then another presence made itself known to me and said she was Michael's Aunt, and she was always with him. These spirits were not the ones responsible for the unusual activity; however, there were still places to investigate.

The team walked down the hall and when someone opened a closed door a small white foggy mist was seen by everyone present. It quickly flew up into the ceiling and disappeared. Upon playback of the video tape in slow motion, the object even leaves a reflection in a mirror in the closet! I felt the presence of two housekeepers in this area, which was close to the servant's quarters and stairs. The ghost of the original owner of the house wanted us to go up to the attic and pulled me in that direction.

Not long after walking into the attic area, Michael, Chris, and I all smelled a cherry tobacco pipe burning. There was an area where the owner had built himself a desk/work area and we surmised that this is where he used to escape from the noise of the household to do his work and smoke his pipe. In those days, it was common for the men to have a special area to smoke. Several photos were taken and some of them showed orbs. I felt a lot of activity here, and the homeowner confirmed that they often heard footsteps in the attic and on the attic stairs.

Attic area—note video camera on the right held by an investigator, and several whitish orbs in the photo around the attic ceiling/roof.

Photo taken of the hallway—note small orb on the wall to the right. Other photos of this same area do not show orbs.

As we passed by the chimney, I was drawn to it and put my hand on it. I could sense carbon monoxide being a health problem for the occupants at some time in the past and that someone became very ill because of this.

Most investigations are not this fruitful. We got high EMF readings in almost every room in the house, most notably in the library, foyer, upstairs bathroom, hall closet and in the attic in places where there were no electronic devices or electric wiring.

Together with the pipe smell, the sounds caught on the digital voice recorder, orbs caught on film, and the fog in the closet- it is my opinion that this house is very haunted, although with quite friendly spirits. The owners wanted to leave the spirits alone since they cause no problems, so we did not ask them to leave.

The Ghost Children

I worked on a missing person case a few years ago involving Lindsey Porter, age 8, and Sam Porter, age 7, who were kidnapped by their father, Dan Porter, in Independence, Missouri in June of 2004. The case was highly publicized, but I didn't know about it until one day six months after their disappearance, when I saw their pictures at the local HY-Vee grocery store. I immediately had a vision, and knew that I was connected to these children somehow. I'd never had that feeling with other missing person notices, or with missing person cases I worked on. I asked my employees about it, and sure enough, one of them was her neighbor and knew the details of the case. I immediately got in contact with the children's mother, Tina Porter, and my daughter and I met with her and her sister.

At our first meeting I went into a light trance and heard Dan talking to a number of people including his sister, mother, brother, neighbors, and friends. Each time he discussed a different set of plans regarding what they were going to do with the children after the kidnapping, so it was extremely confusing as to what actually happened.

Naturally, the mother was anxious to know where her children were and what happened to them. Even though Dan Porter sat in jail with the threat of a prison sentence, he would not tell police what happened. His story changed daily. I even tried to "read" him from a distance, but was not successful in discovering what he had done, likely because he had all kinds of different scenarios in his head.

Not long after our first meeting with Tina Porter, both of my daughters and I started having psychic communication with the two children, but mostly with Lindsey. We got extremely detailed locations and conversations with the people involved. The children told me they were alive and could be located near a bend in a large river and other body of water below ground level, near railroad tracks and an unnamed street. I thought that this meant they were alive and held in some sort of bunker under the ground. When I told their mother this she said it would not be inconceivable because their father was a skilled survivalist, was in the woods often, and could have built something like that easily.

Lindsey spoke to me again and said clearly that she was near an unnamed street, a railroad track, near a bend in a river, and another body of water nearby. I dowsed a map with a pendulum and was pulled to two locations: Arkansas near a river with a bend in it, and the Missouri River near Hannibal, Missouri. The Arkansas location had railroad tracks and an unnamed street, and was near where Dan Porter's mother lived. We thought this must be the location. Lindsey Porter was in contact with me telepathically on and off for months, but never indicated that they were in any trouble. I then contacted the Independence Police detective who was working on this case but he never called me back.

A fourth member of our investigative team then went to a park in Sugar Creek, Missouri because she was 'pulled' to go there. She heard children's voices as if they were playing, but could not locate any children. She didn't think anything about it at the time and did not tell us about it, she just thought they must be ghost children and didn't make any connection to the Porter case, and wasn't alarmed because she often saw or heard ghosts and was very used to doing so.

Then one day in January, I had the sudden urge to visit that same park in Sugar Creek. I had never been there, but was again told by Lindsey to go to that location. My oldest daughter called me that same day and said she wanted to go visit that park and thought it had something to do with the Porter children. Now I was convinced that something was going on.

I went into trance, and Lindsey Porter told me she was there with her brother. So the three of us went to the location, to a spot I've never been. I happened to drive to the exact spot where our fourth team member heard children's voices months before. We all got out and walked to the exact same spot —and felt strongly that we were on to something. I felt strong pull to a location deeper in the woods and said we should go back and get some shovels and dig where I was being pulled. However, upon arriving home my husband suggested that this was probably not a good idea so we decided against it.

Lindsey Porter visited me in my dreams often, showing me where she and her brother were and what they were doing. There were many places they visited. The entire time I thought she was alive because the images were so vivid. I had worked on many missing person cases before this, all were adults, and all were deceased and knew it. The only other case involving a child turned out good because she was found alive at the address I found, but the child did not communicate telepathically, I was just able to find her vibration. So I had no experience with deceased children up to this point.

Several months later, I went in to a trance to work on another case when Lindsey Porter popped in and spoke to me. She said they could see the fireworks from where they were on July 4 on the Missouri River. The next morning I heard banging on my bathroom wall that was so hard it moved the picture on the wall. The picture is a boat on a river. I shared this information with my team and we met to talk about it. We thought: boat = river = Missouri River = spot near the park. So we got out a map of Sugar

Creek and sure enough, there is the bend in the Missouri river, the water works near it, railroad tracks and in unnamed street. All too coincidental.

I did another trance session and spoke with Lindsey Porter, and she showed me what happened. Their father had taken them out to the woods and shot them both and buried them in the ground. He told them that they would all (including their mother) soon be together and that this was the only way.

Lindsey had just come to realize, partly because of our telepathic communication over the months, that she and her brother had passed over and were in spirit form. She said they were both doing OK, but that she felt the need to get this resolved for her family's sake so they could have some peace and move on with their lives, and so that the two of them could move on to other things as they were supposed to do. She said they felt alive, and did not know they had actually left their bodies recently.

I then contacted Tina Porter, but did not tell her what I knew. I asked her to have the FBI contact me so I could tell them what we found, but no one called me back. I asked her to do this a second time, but still no one called me back. I was ready to talk to the FBI or police because we were so certain of our findings. Two days later, on September 9, 2007, the children were found in the exact location that we knew they were. We never got the chance to share that information with the police.

This case was frustrating and very sad, but it taught me a lesson: people, especially children, may not know they have died for some time, and need help to see that and move on. Some ghosts really don't realize they have died because they feel so alive. It also demonstrates that the spirit world can give you detailed information that may be very useful in solving mysteries.

The White Witch of Rose Hall

I traveled to Montego Bay in Jamaica in 2007 and visited Rose Hall, which is operated by the Jamaica National Trust. As soon as my husband and I entered the property, I could feel multiple spirits watching us. The Rose Hall Great House and plantation was built in 1770 by John Palmer, and was the site of horrors for the years that Annie Patterson lived there. Annie was born to an Irish father and English mother, and was brought up in Haiti, where she learned Voodoo from her Haitian nanny. When she was 10 years old her parents mysteriously died, and Annie stayed with her nanny until she was 18.

Annie went to Jamaica in order to find a wealthy husband, and soon married John Palmer, owner of Rose Hall. She often had affairs with her slaves, and often killed them so they couldn't tell anyone. She soon tired of Palmer after six years and poisoned him, then locked up his room, forbidding anyone to enter it. Annie them married two more husbands and killed them, too. She was known to severely punish slaves, and enjoyed watching them being flogged from her bedroom balcony, then dropping them into pits in the dungeon in the basement, where they died of thirst and starvation. No one was allowed to assist these poor souls or they would suffer the same fate. No one knows how many people she killed or had killed.

Annie was eventually strangled to death by the father of her housekeeper, after Annie killed her using Voodoo. The guide told us that Annie's apparition often appears in the mirror of her house when a photo is taken. Sure enough, I took a picture of the mirror and there is a foggy apparition in it. I don't recommend a visit to Rose Hall if you are faint of heart.

CHAPTER 12

66 Famous Haunted Sites to Visit

Most of the sites listed in this section are open to the public. Some have tours, others can be reserved for a night's stay, and some are open daily. I have visited most of these sites myself or they have been recommended by other paranormal investigators. Whether you go during the day or night, take your camera with you and take lots of photos!

The Ghost Hunter's Field Guide

Houses

The Truman Home, Independence, Missouri
223 N Main St, Independence, Missouri
Finished in 1886 by Bess Wallace Truman's maternal grandfather George Porterfield. Called "The Summer White House" and where Truman lived after his marriage to Bess. This is where Harry died in 1972. The home is open to the public daily. Watch out for Harry himself, who often appears sitting at his desk in the living room or walking outside the home and even around old downtown Independence.

Winchester Mystery House- California
525 S Winchester Blvd
San Jose, CA 95128
408-247-2101
www.winchestermysteryhouse.com
Sarah Winchester built what is considered to be the world's oddest mansion because her dead husband told her she and all their descendents were cursed because of the rifle he invented. She was told to build and never stop building. By her death she had 160 rooms in her mansion. Sarah lived alone with her servants, carpenters and the ghosts of all who had died by the Winchester rifle. There have been multiple experiences here by visitors. Open year-round.

Ax Murder House- Villisca Iowa
www.villiscaiowa.com
June 10, 1912 the entire J. B. Moore family were killed by an axe murderer in this house. Visitors have reported hearing sounds of

children laughing, and of apparitions caught on film, falling lamps, and objects moving on their own. Listed on the National Registry of Historic Places. Open for daytime tours and overnight stays.

The Whaley House-San Diego, California
www.whaleyhouse.org
619-297-7511
Whaley house admissions are sold at the museum at 2476 San Diego Avenue on Old Town San Diego. According to the Travel Channel's *America's Most Haunted,* the house is the number one most haunted house in the United States. With its history of the suicide of Violet Whaley in 1885 and the hanging of Yankee Jim James Robinson in 1852 on the spot where the house would be built later, it is no wonder it is haunted. I experienced the ghost of a young girl in the back garden while visiting this site in 2004, the apparition of a man in the front hallway, ghosts of children in the upper level of the home, and an angry male spirit near the stairway to the second floor.

The Deane House
Calgary, Alberta, Canada
403-569-7747
www.fortcalgary.com/deane.htm
Multiple deaths have occurred in the home over the years including a suicide of a 14-year old boy in 1933, a murder/suicide in 1952, and other natural deaths. There are unconfirmed tales of murders, here, too. Staff and visitors report smelling pipe smoke from no known source, disconnected phones ringing, and apparitions of Native Americans. Open Mon- Fri year round and available for private functions.

The Ghost Hunter's Field Guide

The Vaile Mansion- Independence, Missouri
1500 N Liberty Street
816-229-8923
www.vailemansion.org
The haunted Vaile Mansion was built in 1881 by Colonel Harvey Vaile. Reportedly, Mrs. Vaile took an overdose of morphine and died here in 1894. Later, the home was used as an asylum and sanitarium and the cages were people were kept are still in the basement. The Vaile Mansion also served as a rest home for a time. Spirits and ghostly activity have occurred over the years in several rooms in the house, on the grounds, and in the neighborhood. Operated by the Vaile Victorian Society and open year-round for tours and events.

Ordsall Hall- Greater Manchester, England
0161-794-4711
www.salford.gov.uk/ordsallhall.htm
This 750-year old structure has been the subject of many haunting investigations, including the TV show Most Haunted. The story is that the White Lady, who appears in the Star Chamber or Great hall is Margaret Radclyffe, who died here in 1599 following the death of her twin brother, Alexander or possibly that of Viviana Radclyffe. A ghost has also been spotted walking the grounds in the middle of the night, and staff experiences noises, objects moving, and doors closing on their own. The hall has ghost cams set up that you can visit on the internet.

Cemeteries

Bachelors Grove Cemetery– Midloathian, Illinois
www.bachelorsgrove.com
Located on the Southwest side of Chicago. Over the years this place has been cursed with more than 100 documented reports of paranormal phenomena, from actual apparitions to glowing balls of light.

Hill Park– Independence, Missouri
2099 S Hardy Ave
Independence, MO
The burial site of Frank James and his wife and at least two confederate soldiers. A misty figure is often seen crossing over the hill at sunset. The small cemetery is located at the very back of the park at the top of the hill.

Mound Grove Cemetery– Independence, Missouri
1818 N River Blvd.
Independence, MO
A full-body apparition of a young woman in white floats along the main road inside the cemetery, and a dark figure of a man appear in a dip on the same road. Closes at sunset so don't go after dark.

Woodlawn Cemetery– Independence, Missouri
701 N Noland Rd.
Independence, MO
A very large cemetery where voices and whispering can sometimes be heard. Also near the "Noland Road Lady in Grey," an apparition that walks on Noland Road near the cemetery day or night.

Marie Laveau's Grave– New Orleans, Louisiana

Home of the most famous ghost of Voodoo Queen Marie Laveau, where she can be seen walking in St. Louis Cemetery No.1 even today. I've visited several of the cemeteries in New Orleans and they are ALL haunted!

Hospitals

Glore Psychiatric Museum
3406 Frederick Avenue
St. Joseph, Missouri 64508
www.stjosephmuseum.org/glore.htm
800-530-8866
Chronicles the 130-year history of the "State lunatic Asylum No.2" which is haunted by several restless spirits. Tours available.

Waverly Hills Sanatorium– Louisville, Kentucky
502-933-2142
www.therealywaverlyhills.com
A TB sanatorium opened in 1910. There have been many sightings of ghosts including a small girl running, and a boy with a leather ball. Also smells of baking waft thru the air. On the fifth floor disembodied voices demand visitors to "get out". Open for tours and investigators.

Bed and Breakfast/Inns

Myrtles Plantation– Louisiana
7747 U S Hwy 61
St. Francisville, LA 70775

800-809-0565

www.themyrtlesplantation.com

Restaurant and tours. As you visit this 1776 plantation built by General
David Bradford don't be surprised if you see full-body apparitions or handprints in the mirrors, hear footsteps on the stairs, and more. Reported to be one of the most haunted houses in the United States.

Lemp Mansion Restaurant and Inn—St. Louis, Missouri

3322 DeMerit Place

St. Louis, Missouri 63118

314-664-8024

www.lempmansion.com

Considered one of the ten most haunted places in America, this 1868 mansion built by Jacob Feickert, and purchased by William Lemp in 1876. Several deaths occurred in the house due to natural causes and suicides and many ghost stories abound about this place. There are six ghosts here. Open to the public as a bed and breakfast, restaurant, and dinner theatre. Paranormal tours are available.

Lizzie Bordon Bed and Breakfast Museum– Fall River, Mass.

92 Second Street

Fall River, Massachusetts 02721

508-605-6333

www.lizzie-bordon.com

This is a beautiful fully restored Victorian home and site of the gruesome axe murders of Andrew Bordon in the sitting room and Abby Bordon in her bedroom on August 4, 1892. Lizzie Bordon, daughter of Andrew, was the prime suspect but was found not guilty at her trial. Several paranormal investigators have captured ghosts on film and EVPs on recorders. Sleep over night here or take one of the daily tours.

Hotels and Restaurants

The Stanley Hotel– Colorado
333 E Wonder View Ave
Estes Park, CO 80517-9665
970-586-3371
www.stanleyhotel.com
This very haunted hotel, which opened in 1909, inspired the Stephen King novel "The Shining." Book room 217, which is where King stayed or anywhere on floor 4, which was the servant's quarters. Flora Stanley, the wife of the hotel owner is among the many ghosts that haunt the place. Open year-round.

The Hotel Savoy- Kansas City, Missouri
219 W 9th Street
Kansas City, MO
www.hotelsavoy.net
816-842-3575
1888 brick building haunted by several ghosts who were upset by renovations in the 1980's. Watch out for Betsy Ward, who died in a bathtub in the 1880's and Fred Lightner haunting his former apartment. Open to the public.

The Ghost Hunter's Field Guide

The Hyatt– Kansas City, Missouri
2345 McGee Street
Kansas City, Missouri
816-421-1234
www.crowncenter.hyatt.com
Site of the terrible Hyatt Regency walkway collapse in 1981 which killed 114 people during a tea dance. One of the floors is closed due to multiple sightings of ghosts there, however ghosts have been spotted in the ballroom, elevator, lobby, and on several floors. The staff does not talk about it, so just keep your eye out if you spend the night there.

The 1886 Crescent Hotel and Spa– Eureka Springs, Arkansas
75 Prospect Avenue
Eureka Springs, AR 72632
877-342-9766
www.crescent-hotel.com
Room 218 is the most active spot for paranormal activity, likely because one of the Irish stone masons working on the structure in the 1880's fell to his death here. However, I saw a ghost cat in the lobby who walked through the glass doors, and other people have reported sightings, loud noises, and poltergeist activity throughout the hotel. Two friends of mine even had UFO sightings from their balconies. Definitely worth a visit.

The Sagamore– Bolton Landing, New York
110 Sagamore Road
Bolton Landing, NY 12814
833-385-6221
www.thesagamore.com
Located on a private island on Lake George. While dining in the

Trillium you may be visited by a couple who descend from the second floor and take a seat in the restaurant's reception room. Or visit the hotel's second restaurant, Mr. Brown's, where you may see an apparition of a tall woman dressed in white evening attire.

Jekyll Island Club Hotel– Jekyll Island, Georgia
371 Riverview Drive
Jekyll Island, GA 61527
www.jekyllclub.com
Samuel Spencer still haunts his room at the hotel. Spencer was president of the Southern Railroad Company and had a morning routine of reading the Wall Street Journal while drinking coffee. He died in 1906 in a railroad accident, but still drinks his morning coffee in his room today.

Courthouse Exchange Restaurant– Independence, Missouri
113 W Lexington
Independence, Missouri
Haunted by prankster ghost children in the bar and restaurant who are very active. The manager told me the ghosts play a "dime game" and leave several dimes, always face-up, on tables and the bar nightly and often leave the TV turned to the cartoon channel on in the morning. A ghost girl has been spotted by patrons on a number of occasions.

Theatres

The Music Hall- Kansas City, Missouri
301 W 13th Street
Kansas City, Missouri

If you attend a concert there, watch out for several ghosts who haunt, especially inside the theatre where they sit in chairs. Most witnesses think they are looking at a real person until the apparition disappears. No tours are available.

Landers Theater– Springfield, Missouri
311 E Walnut
Springfield, Missouri 65806
www.springfieldlittetheatre.org
417-869-3869 (office)
Built in 1909 and still used as a civic theatre today, the theater has a history of tragic deaths and ghosts that haunt. The beautiful theatre is on the National Register of Historic Places.

Lincoln Theater- Decatur, Illinois
Listen as you enter the theater and you may hear ghostly footsteps, inexplicable sounds, and even feel icy cold chills that appear and disappear without explanation. Lincoln Theater is a glorious place—come meet restless phantoms of those whose lives ended on this spot, some before the theater existed.

Bobby Mackey's Music World-Wilder, Kentucky
Occult rituals, trials, strange visits to women five months pregnant and many other delights visit you in this strange house with just ads strange a history.

Coleman Theatre– Miami, Oklahoma
On Historic Route 66 in northeastern Oklahoma. A beautiful restored theatre, the Coleman is famous for its ghostly residents. The theatre is haunted by a little boy named Stuart, who likes to hold on to lady's legs, making them cold. You can also smell men's

cologne and pipes at times, and walk into cold spots.

Syracuse Landmark Theater-Syracuse, New York
362 S Salina St, Syracuse, NY
315-475-7980
www.landmarktheatre.org
This 1928 theatre was renovated in 1978 and shortly after the apparition of a pale lady, and an electrician named Oscar Rau started haunting it. The theater is on the National Register of Historic Places

Battlefields/Forts

Gettysburg Battlefield– Southern Pennsylvania
Gettysburg National Military Park
97 Taneytown Rd.
Gettysburg, PA 17325
717-334-1124
www.nps.gov/gett
The bloodiest battle of the Civil War was fought here July 1 –3, 1863. Over 51,000 soldiers were killed, wounded, or captured on this spot. The battle spilled over in to the town, where ghostly apparitions of men, women, and children have been sighted. The battlefield is one of the most haunted sites in America. Don't be surprised if you see reinactors in uniform only to find out that they can walk through walls and trees.

Antietam Battlefield, Maryland
5831 Dunker Church Road
Sharpsburg, MD 21782

www.nps.gov/anti
The second bloodiest battle of the Civil War was fought here on September 17, 1832. 23,000 soldiers died on that day, which lead to President Lincoln's issuance of the Emancipation Proclamation. Visitors report seeing orbs and apparitions, hearing gunfire and cannon, and seeing strange blue lights in the battlefield, nearby houses and the cemetery.

Chickamouga, and Chattanooga National Military Park– Eastern Tennessee and northern Georgia.
423-821-7786
www.nps.gov/chch
Chickamauga Battlefield is located near Fort Oglethorpe. Lookout Mountain Battlefield is located at the end of East Brow Road near Point Park. Said to be very haunted by visitors ever since the Civil war battle in September of 1863. Visitors have taken photographs of ghost horses and men, and have seen apparitions of tall, dark entities.

The Alamo– San Antonio, Texas
300 Alamo Plaza
San Antonio, Texas 78299
www.thealamo.org
Since March 6, 1836 the ghosts of Jim Bowie and Davy Crockett along with many others have purportedly haunted this site.

Little Bighorn– Montana
Little Bighorn National Monument
Exit 510 off I-90 Hwy 212
Crow Agency, MT 59022

406-638-3217
www.nps.gov.libi
The site of Custer's Last Stand in June 1876, and where reports of shadows, mists, fog, apparitions, and Indian chanting and war cries can be seen and heard here.

Valley Forge– Pennsylvania
Valley Forge Convention and Visitors Bureau
600 W Germantown Pike, Suite 130
Plymouth Meeting, PA 19462
800-441-3549
www.valleyforge.org
The site where General Washington's Continental Army camped for six months from December 1777 to June 1778 during severe conditions and bitter, long winter, and where may ghosts have been seen and heard.

Fort Osage-Missouri
107 Osage Street
Sibley, MO 64088
816-650-3278
www.fortosagehs.com
The second U.S. outpost built following the Louisiana Purchase, a site chosen by William Clark in 1808. The Fort housed soldiers guarding the new territory and acted as a stop for settlers heading west. The current fort is an exact duplicate of the original. Current workers and visitors report sightings and interaction with soldiers and Indians.

The Ghost Hunter's Field Guide

Cold Harbor Battlefield– Richmond, Virginia
Five miles southeast of Mechanicsville on route 156
804-226-1981
www.nps.gov/rich
Ulysses S Grant was in command at this battle that was fought between May 31 and June 12, 1864. 16,000 men died or were wounded. Visitors report encounters with apparitions of solders, strange lights, the sounds of horses and cannon, and orbs and mist captured on film.

When going to a battlefield, check ahead for opening hours and directions. Don't depend on GPS– sometimes it is not correct.

Schools

Note: get permission before going into closed or non-public buildings.

Central Missouri State University– Warrensburg, Missouri
Ghosts have been reported in Deimer Hall, Hawkins Hall, Houts/Hosey Hall, North Ellis, and Yeater Hall. Yeater is the most famous for apparitions—I know firsthand since I lived in that hall. Besides things happening inside, you may also get a glimpse of a female ghost in a third-floor window. Get permission before you go inside since these are dormitories.

Kansas State University– Manhattan, Kansas
Pi Cappa Phi fraternity and Gamma Phi Beta sorority houses are reportedly haunted by ghosts.

The Ghost Hunter's Field Guide

Stephens College-Columbia, Missouri
Senior Hall, where the ghost of Sarah June Wheeler searches for the ghost of Confederate Soldier Isaac Johnson. They both perished on the site or nearby.

St. Joseph's college– Emmitsburg, Maryland
A former women's college that was used a hospital during the Civil War. The apparition of Saint Mother Seton is often seen in the corridors accompanied by the ghost of a doctor.

Lourdes High School– Chicago, Illinois
4034 West 57th Street, Chicago, Illinois
Students, teachers and visitors report hearing music, talking, and ghostly footsteps when the halls are quiet.

Decatur High School– Decatur, Alabama
Apparitions floating down the hall and footsteps in silent corridors have been reported by students and teachers here.

The Music Academy– Independence, Missouri
Look up at the third floor windows from the street where you might catch a glimpse of a young girl ghost. She has been reported by multiple witnesses.

Henderson State University– Arkadelphia, Arkansas
Home of "The Black Lady," a ghost of a woman who returns during dances at the school and may be the ghost of a young woman who committed suicide there.

Reynolds College– Denver, Colorado
The ghost of Madge Reynolds has been seen in her bedroom in this

historic house, where she died after returning from a horseback ride with her lover Fred Bonfils.

Eastern Illinois University– Charleston, Illinois
The ghost of Mary, a counselor who was killed by a custodian on the 3rd floor of Pemberton Hall in the 1920's, often drifts from room to room checking on the girls there.

Gorman School– Lebec, California
The school was built on the site of a farm where a 12-year-old girl was killed by her father's tractor. Her body was laid to rest under the state in the school auditorium and often appears to people and sometimes speaks to them.

Prisons and Jails

Alcatraz-San Francisco California
www.nps.gov/alcatraz
First a fortress (1850-1934), then a prison (1934-1963), and the American Indian occupation (1964 –1971). From its naming in 1775 Alcatraz has been host to prisoners- Confederate soldiers to our countries most hardened criminals like Al Capone and Robert Stroud. Tours available to the public. Only accessible by ferry.

1859 Jackson County Jail– Independence, Missouri
Includes the Marshal's House, which is also haunted. Former housing to thousands of men, women, and child prisoners during the Civil War and after, including Frank James and William Clark Quantrill until it closed in 1933. Much ghostly activity has been reported here and we experienced this during our own visit.

Apparitions appear, ghosts fight with each other, cold spots abound, and visitors report invisible hands touching their shoulders. Open to the public year round. I don't recommend this for children due to the high likelihood of a paranormal encounter.

Eastern State Penitentiary– Pennsylvania
2124 Fairmount Ave.
Philadelphia, PA 19130
215-236-5111
www.easternstate.org
A massive 1829 gothic structure in Philadelphia's Fairmount neighborhood and former home to Al Capone, Slick Willie Sutton, and thousands of other prisoners who lived and died there. U.S. National Register of Historic Places. Open to the public for tours year-round.

The Tower of London
0870 756 6060
www.hrp.org.uk
This 1,000 year old structure is home to the ghosts of Henry VI, Thomas a Becket, Sir Walter Raleigh and Anne Boleyn, who all died there. Public executions were held on Tower Green, including two of Henry VIII's wives Anne Boleyn and Catherine Howard. The White Tower built by William the Conqueror around 1100 now houses a display of armory. I encountered spirits in the tower while visiting in 2005. Open year-round to the public.

Other Famous Haunted Places

(Not in Alphabetical Order)

Bell Witch Cave- Adams, Tennessee

The Bell Witch Cave & Canoe Rental
430 Keysburg Road, Adams, TN 37010
615-696-3055
www.bellwitchcave.com
The story starts in 1817 with the family of a local farmer named John Bell. John Bell was plagued for by a mysterious and violent spirit for nearly four years. The haunting included spectral creatures, disembodied voices, unbelievable violence and even resulted in the death of John Bell, all at the hands of the infamous Bell Witch, many of whom believe moved to this cave after leaving the Bell residence.

Dracula's Castle or Castle Bran- Wlachia, Transylvania

Situated in the remote Carpathian Mountains in Romania, Bran Castle was home to Vlad the Impaler, who impaled thousands of victims at a time during his reign of terror. Very difficult to access, so only the very adventurous should plan to visit.

The Catacombs– Paris, France

The home to thousands of the dead since the late 1800's and the site of many ghostly experiences. Do not go without a guide or you risk getting lost forever in the maze of catacombs under the city. Check with local tour operators for information. The entrance to the Paris Catacombs is located across the street from the Denfert Rochereau Metro station.

Laularie House– New Orleans, Louisiana
1140 Royal Street
New Orleans, Louisiana
Visitors report seeing and hearing the long-dead slaves and original owners of this home as they frantically try to put out the fire that killed them long ago. Open to the public.

Underground Vaults- Edinburgh, Scotland
Under the streets of the city lie vaults that were used 200 years ago by businesses, residences, and workshops. Later, the homeless used the vaults and it is suspected that the famous Burke and Hare killed homeless and sold the bodies to the teaching hospitals. The ghosts here are very aggressive and have actually caused physical harm to people. Not for children.

The Coliseum– Rome, Italy
This 2000-year-old structure was home to Gladiator battles to the death, and religious persecution where thousands lost their lives when attacked by lions and tigers. Visitors have reported cold spots, being touched or pushed, hearing talking, and crying along with animal noises.

The New Castle (Black Gate and Keep)- England
Newcastle-upon-Tyne
0191 231 2700
www.newcaslte-antiquaries.org.
Castle built by Henry 11 in 1168– 78
Hundreds of dead were moved from a graveyard in 1172 in order to allow for the new castle to be built. Many paranormal investigators have reported seeing spirits here. Open for tours.

The Ghost Hunter's Field Guide

Edinburgh Castle– Scotland
www.edinburghcastle.gov.uk

A fortress built in the 12th century, home of dungeons used for torture and imprisonment over the centuries and home to spirits now. The vaults used to quarantine victims of the plague are reportedly haunted, and visitors often hear the screams of spirits. Open to the public.

Chillingham Castle– England
2 Market Street
Alnwich, Northcumberland NE66 65N
01668 215 359
www.chillingham-catle.com

Visit this 13th century castle and you may see the "blue boy" who haunts the Pink Room where his body was found bricked up in a 10-foot thick wall, Lady Mary, or hear the cries of the tortured souls in the dungeons or of the eight executions of famous people who were hung, drawn and quartered. Open to the public May— October.

Union Station- Kansas City, Missouri
30 West Pershing, Rd.
Kansas City, MO 64105
816-221-5111

Site of the Kansas City Massacre. Built in 1914, Union Station was once a thriving railway station for passengers and freight. Now fully restored and open to the public. Ghosts carrying bags have been reported in the old lobby, on the railroad tracks, in Pierponts restaurant and in the Historical Room above Pierponts. I heard a ghost in the ladies room, and saw an apparition in the main lobby while visiting in 2009. This was the site of the 1933 Massacre of federal agents by Pretty Boy Floyd, Vernon Miller, and Adam Richetti to free prisoner Frank Nash. Open year-round.

The Queen Mary– Long Beach, California
1126 Queen's Highway
Long Beach, CA 90802
877-342-0742

This 1936 ship has been turned into a hotel for guests to the Long Beach area. The ship made over 1,000 Atlantic crossings and it is estimated that almost 50 people lost their lives on the vessel. During WWII the ocean liner collided with the Curacoa from Britain, which was split in two. Because of strict orders the Queen Mary could not stop to rescue the 338 men who perished as a result of the accident. Open to the public for tours and overnight stays in the hotel.

The White House– Washington, DC
It is rumored that at least 20 ghost haunt the White House, with Abe Lincoln's bedroom being the most haunted. Even Queen Elizabeth **saw** the ghost of Lincoln during a visit there. Ghosts have been reported in all rooms and on the lawn, but the most haunted rooms are not open to the public. To get tickets, contact your member of Congress and request tickets to tour the White House several months in advance of your visit. Tours are self guided and begin at 7:30 a.m. and run until 11:30 a.m. Tuesday through Saturday. Call 202-456-7041.

The Capital Building—Washington, DC
Constitution Avenue.
www.visitthecapital.gov
Open from 8:30 a.m. to 4:30 p.m. Monday—Saturday except for

The Ghost Hunter's Field Guide

Edinburgh Castle– Scotland
www.edinburghcastle.gov.uk

A fortress built in the 12th century, home of dungeons used for torture and imprisonment over the centuries and home to spirits now. The vaults used to quarantine victims of the plague are reportedly haunted, and visitors often hear the screams of spirits. Open to the public.

Chillingham Castle– England
2 Market Street
Alnwich, Northcumberland NE66 65N
01668 215 359
www.chillingham-catle.com

Visit this 13th century castle and you may see the "blue boy" who haunts the Pink Room where his body was found bricked up in a 10-foot thick wall, Lady Mary, or hear the cries of the tortured souls in the dungeons or of the eight executions of famous people who were hung, drawn and quartered. Open to the public May—October.

Union Station- Kansas City, Missouri
30 West Pershing, Rd.
Kansas City, MO 64105
816-221-5111

Site of the Kansas City Massacre. Built in 1914, Union Station was once a thriving railway station for passengers and freight. Now fully restored and open to the public. Ghosts carrying bags have been reported in the old lobby, on the railroad tracks, in Pierponts restaurant and in the Historical Room above Pierponts. I heard a ghost in the ladies room, and saw an apparition in the main lobby while visiting in 2009. This was the site of the 1933 Massacre of

The Ghost Hunter's Field Guide

federal agents by Pretty Boy Floyd, Vernon Miller, and Adam Richetti to free prisoner Frank Nash. Open year-round.

The Queen Mary– Long Beach, California
1126 Queen's Highway
Long Beach, CA 90802
877-342-0742

This 1936 ship has been turned into a hotel for guests to the Long Beach area. The ship made over 1,000 Atlantic crossings and it is estimated that almost 50 people lost their lives on the vessel. During WWII the ocean liner collided with the Curacoa from Britain, which was split in two. Because of strict orders the Queen Mary could not stop to rescue the 338 men who perished as a result of the accident. Open to the public for tours and overnight stays in the hotel.

The White House– Washington, DC
It is rumored that at least 20 ghost haunt the White House, with Abe Lincoln's bedroom being the most haunted. Even Queen Elizabeth **saw** the ghost of Lincoln during a visit there. Ghosts have been reported in all rooms and on the lawn, but the most haunted rooms are not open to the public. To get tickets, contact your member of Congress and request tickets to tour the White House several months in advance of your visit. Tours are self-guided and begin at 7:30 a.m. and run until 11:30 a.m. Tuesday through Saturday. Call 202-456-7041.

The Capital Building—Washington, DC
Constitution Avenue.
www.visitthecapital.gov
Open from 8:30 a.m. to 4:30 p.m. Monday—Saturday except for

holidays. Reservations must be made in advance through your representative or senator, or book online at the capital website (above).

Visit the Capital Building while in DC and you may see the ghost of John Adams walking around along with Vice-President Henry Wilson, President James Garfield, General Jon Alexander, a custodian, and others. A black cat (called the Demon Cat) is sometimes sighted before a tragedy or administration changes.

Old Salem: Salem, Massachusetts
Site of the Salem witch trials in 1692 where the court hung 20 women and crushed one man to death with stones. Reported haunted sites are the Ward House which is haunted by the ghosts of Sheriff Corwin and Giles Corey. Corwin is buried in the cellar. The YMCA pool is haunted by a swimmer who died there. The Hawthorne Hotel elevator and sixth floor are haunted by murdered ghosts, and Gallows Hill is reported to be haunted by the "witches" who died there. During a visit by the QUEST team we encountered full apparitions in windows of buildings, and at the old jail. During a walk through the town graveyard a ghost yanked my purse off of me and broke the strap.

Plymouth, Massachusetts
Reported to be haunted at Clapp Park, Cortage Park, the Spooner House Museum, and the State Forest. While driving the streets in Plymouth, sometimes spelled Plimoth, I felt many spirits in the town. No wonder, this is one of the oldest settlements in the U.S. The Spooner House Museum is worth visiting, haunted or not.

Tombstone, Arizona

Reported to be one of the most haunted towns in the world. Tombstone was a boomtown from 1877 1889 when silver was discovered and the site of many bloody shootouts, including the famous O.K. Corral incident. The ghost of Marshal Fred White has been seen. White was the first marshal of Tombstone. A man in a long black frock coat has been seen near the site where Virgil Earp was ambushed and shot in the arm. Also spied on the streets is a woman in a long white dress. More than 40 men died in fires in 1881 and 1882 and some have been seen walking the streets while the unexplained smell of smoke is noted. Visitors also report getting ghosts on camera. Be sure to visit Big Nose Kate's Saloon and restaurant where "The Swamper" may come up from the basement or you may feel a ghostly presence at the very bar where Wyatt Earp, Doc Holliday had drinks. www.bignosekate.com.

Clark Street– Chicago, Illinois

Site of the famous Saint Valentine's Day Massacre in 1929 and the site where 812 people died under the Clark Street bridge when the Eastland boat capsized in 1915. Cries can still be heard under the bridge.

Mammoth Cave National Park– Kentucky

The largest natural cave in the world. Over 150 reports of ghostly activity since the cave's discovery in 1978 and very active today. At least five spirits haunt the site.

San Antonio, Texas

Another very haunted site, San Antonio is one of the oldest cities in the U.S. and has a long, rich history. The Alamo, the Railroad tracks, the Sheraton Gunter Hotel, and Menger Hotel are reported to be haunted. After the battle of the Alamo, Mexican troops saw full apparitions and heard them yelling for the men to leave. Moaning sounds and shadows still appear at this site. Just south of San Antonio near the San Juan Mission is the site of the most famous ghost legend in Texas. Ten children were killed when a train hit a school bus in the 1930's or 40's, and since then ghost children push cars uphill at this intersection. Supposedly, if you stop your car right over the railroad tracks and shift into neutral, the car will be pushed out of the way uphill by the ghosts of the children.

The Real 'Blair Witch' Ghosts, Burkitsville, Maryland
The movie was fiction, but the site is not.
Since 1735, people have been talking about the strange goings on around Burkitsville. According to some the community has been terrorized by the "Schnellgeister," the German word for "fast sprit." Described as half-reptile with octopus limbs and half bird with a metallic beak and sharp teeth, the "Snallygaster" can fly, capture people, and suck their blood. Other animal spirits and ghosts haunt the town, which housed 17 Civil War hospitals. The hospitals were homes and the old tannery used for the purpose. Stories of Civil War ghosts abound. The tannery site is haunted today. If you park your car there overnight you may find footprints from soldier's boots on it in the morning.

CHAPTER 13

Paranormal Radio and TV Shows

The following are current radio and television shows that often cover ghosts and the paranormal.

The Ghost Hunter's Field Guide

Paranormal Radio

Coast to Coast AM with hosts George Noory, Ian Punnett and Art Bell. Currently the most popular talk show on the paranormal. The website iswww.coasttocoastam.com. Live streaming audio (and video) available. Also on XM radio.

UFO Traffic Reports with hosts Roger Marsh and Michael Rambacher, includes interesting paranormal investigations and UFO reports. www.blogtalkradio.com/tremontavenue.

Blogtalkradio: Visit www.blogtalkradio.com and click on the "Paranormal" category to see many radio shows listed.

Nightwatch with host Todd Sheets, is the home of the Nightwatchers paranormal investigative group. www.nightwatchradio.com. Live streaming audio, and through affiliates.

Nightsearch is MUFON Tennessee state director Eddie Middleton's popular paranormal show in the South. The website is www.nightsearch.net. The call-in line is 901-365-1430.

Darkness Radio with David Schrader. www.ktlkfm.com or www.darkessradio.com

Sightings with Jeff Rense is one of the most popular and long-running paranormal radio shows. Real audio and archives are at www.sightings.com.

Paranormal Awareness radio show with author Dr. Hans Holzer. www.paranormalawarenessradioshow.net.

Anomaly Radio with multiple hosts and various topics. www.anomalyradio.com

PsiTalk: Internet web station hosting Dreamland, Ghostly Talk, Jerry pippin, Strange Days, and more. www.psitalk.com

Alabama ParaSpiritual Research Radio with Dr .Jimmy Lowery and Heather Lowery. www.apsrradio.

Paranormal Alaska Radio with Neelie and Tony of IOPIA. www.blocktalkradio.com/alaskaparanormal

Crossroads Paranormal Radio with hosts Kris and Sheila. www.insightbb.com/~crossroadsparanormal/cpr.htm

Tuesday After Twilight international paranormal talk radio. www.tuesdayaftertwilight.com

Ghostly Talk on Sunday nights with Doug "Skizz" and Scott L. . www.ghostlytalk.com

Planet Paranormal talk radio with multiple hosts and programs. www.planetparanormal.com

White Noise Radio paranormal talk radio from the UK. www.whitenoiseradio.webs.com

The Unexplained World talk radio show with Ed and Annette. Www.theunexplainedworld.com.

The Paracast talk radio with Gene Steinberg and Greg Bishop. www.theparacast.com.

The Ghost Hunter's Field Guide

Paranormal TV Shows

Ghost Hunters TV Show with Jason and Grant and the Atlantic Paranormal Society (TAPS) team. On the SyFy channel. www.syfy.com/gh

Ghost Adventures TV show with Zac Bagans, Nick Groff, and Aaron Goodwin investigate while being locked up at the location overnight. On the Travel Channel. www.travelchannel.com/TV_Shows/Ghost_Adventures.

Paranormal State TV show with Ryan Buell and the Paranormal Research Society. Airs on A&E. www.aetv.com/paranormal-state

Ghost Lab TV show with Brad and Barry Klinge and Everyday Paranormal. Airs on the Discovery channel. www.disc.discovery.com/tv/ghost-lab/ghost-lab.html

Ghost Hunters International TV show is a spin-off of Ghost Hunters. On the SyFy channel.

Most Haunted TV show on the Travel Channel with Yvette Fielding and a team of investigators. www.livingtv.co.uk/shows/most-haunted-the-live-series.

Paranormal Cops TV reality show with real-life Chicago police officers by day who work as paranormal investigators at night. www.aetv.com/paranormal-cops/index.jsp

Paranormal TV from the Unexplained World. Live broadcasts and video on demand. www.theunesplainedworld.com.

CHAPTER 14

Resources

EMF Detectors:
http://www.trifield.com/EMF_meter.htm
www.ghosthunterstore.com
www.lessemf.com

Increase your psychic abilities, learn to dowse or go on a ghost hunting expedition: Check with QUEST for classes held every fall in Kansas City and for her scheduled conference lectures and ghost hunts. Website: www.ufokc.4mg.com or e-mail margiekay06@yahoo.com

Meditation CD's:
Rhythmic Medicine (Janalea Hoffman)
www.rhythmicmedicine.com 913-851-5100 or
EOC Institute: www.eocinstitute.org or
MeditiationTransformation:www.meditationtransformation.com

Laser Thermometers:
Laser Thermometers: Laserthermometers.net 1-800-334-9291
Professional Equipment:
www.professionalequipment.com 1-800-334-9291

Digital Voice Recorders:
www.recorders.com 1-800-512-251-1302
www.shop.com

Infrared Monoculars and Binoculars:
www.nightvisionbinoculars.com 1-866-310-8398
www.shop.com

Digital still and video cameras:
Sony: www.sonystyle.com 1-877-865-7669

Canon: www.usa.canon.com

Kodak: www.kodak.com

Best Buy has a good selection of cameras

Reviews of Digital Cameras: *Check this out before you buy!*

www.reviews.cnet.com

Hypnosis Certification: And a list of certified hypnotists

www.ozarkmt.com

> *HINT: Check on E-bay (www.ebay.com) and Craig's List (www.craigslist.com) for great deals on cameras and other equipment. Be sure to get a warranty on new equipment.*

The Ghost Hunter's Field Guide

More Resources

Public libraries are a wealth of information for research. If you need to check the history of a site, check your library for newspaper articles and books on the history of the area.

Old newspaper archives can be found at NewspaperArchive.com for a fee, or visit Google News Archives at news.google.com/archivesearch, and XooxieAnswers.com for free archive searches.

For local family information and photos visit Ancestry.com, Genealogy.com, and cyndislist.com.

For Civil War Records, visit www.nors.us/civilrecords and for Revolutionary War Records visit www.dar.org.

Visit your local county website for property and land information, vital statistics, criminal, and tax information, which may provide more information about the site you are investigating.

CHAPTER 15

Glossary of Paranormal Terms

Agent: A person who is the focus of poltergeist activity.

Akashic Record: Mystical knowledge encoded in a non-physical plane. Also described as a library Accessible through astral projection or consciousness projection, some clairvoyants believe that the Akashic Record is held in the rings of Saturn.

Amulet: An object, such as a stone, or necklace thought to have the power to offer protection.

Anomalous: 1: inconsistent with or deviating from what is usual, normal, or expected: irregular, unusual.

Apparition: The full or partial visible manifestation of a spirit, which often appears as translucent or foggy, but may also appear solid.

Asport: A physical object that a spirit teleports to a different location or makes disappear.

Astral Body: The body that a living person uses to travel in during an involuntary "out of body" experience, often while sleeping or in a deep trance or during intentional "astral projection." While in the astral body, the person can feel objects and hear and see very well.

Astral Plane: A higher dimensional plane that the astral body travels in, and may also be where ghosts exist or travel through.

Astral Projection: When a person purposely and intentionally leaves their physical body via the astral body.

Aura: The field of energy, thought to come from the physical and subtle bodies of a living person, animal, or plant. The auras of people are more complex than other living things. Some clairvoyants can see one or more layers of the aura.

Automatic Writing: The ability to channel a spirit or entity by writing messages without conscious control or memory of what is being written by using a pen or pencil, or typing.

Automatism: An unconscious or involuntary muscular movement theoretically caused by spirits.

Autoscopy: The image of one's body looking back at themselves from a position outside the physical body.

Ball Lightning: A rare form of lighting in the shape of a ball, thought to consist of ionized gas or plasma. Ball lightning only lasts a short time.

Banshee: A Scottish and Irish legend, a female wailing spirit that appears to be in two places at the same time, and is an omen of impending death, especially for those whose surnames beginning with "Mac" and "O."

Channeling: The method a medium uses to contact and relay information to others, often during a séance session.

Clairaudient: A person who can hear voices of the dead or other sounds, or hear a living person speaking who is not within normal hearing range.

Clairsentient: A psychic who can sense or "feel" the presence of something or someone, or who knows something without seeing or hearing it.

Clairvoyant: A person who can see ghosts, see through walls, see far-away locations or past and future events by using their mind or "third eye".

Cold spot: A specific area that is much colder than the surrounding space. An authentic cold spot cannot be explained by drafts, air ducts, or other natural phenomena.

Collective Apparition: When more than one person sees the same apparition or phenomena, often from different locations.

Crisis Apparition: An apparition that is seen just prior to an event that could cause serious injury or death.

Deja' vu: The impression of having experienced something before, often with complete recollection of what is coming next.

Demon: An evil entity, often associated with demonic possession, who has never incarnated into a human body, and who purportedly works with the devil. It is unusual to encounter a real demon.

Digital Camera: A type of filmless camera used successfully in ghost hunting. It is believed that digital cameras capture more of the light spectrum than is normally seen by the human eye.

Direct Voice Phenomenon or DVP: Voice of a spirit that is audible to all or most people doing an investigation or séance.

Doppelganger: The exact mirror image of a person, which is considered to be very negative. May also be the same person in a different time.

Dowsing: The ancient practice of using a pendulum, L-rods, Y-branches, or similar device in order to access the super-conscious mind and locate minerals, water, lost items, or in this case, ghosts.

Draft: Some investigators have success hearing spirits speak through things that cause draft such as chimneys, vents, or tubes.

Earthbound: A ghost or spirit that was unable to cross over to the other side at the time of death and is stuck on earth.

Ectoplasm: An ethereal lifelike substance associated with spirit manifestations, and associated in the 1900's with the ability of a medium to produce ectoplasm. Now ectoplasm refers to fog and mists that have no natural explanation.

Electronic Voice Phenomenon: Sounds or voices of a paranormal source, usually obtained on a voice recorder or video tape.

Elementals: Earth spirits, sprites, fairies, elves, gnomes, and other non-human beings that may exist on the earth and are inter-dimensional.

EMF Detector or Magnetometer: A device used to detect electro-magnetic fields.

Entity: A being other than a living human being, often associated with dark energies.

The Ghost Hunter's Field Guide

Extra Sensory Perception or ESP: Perception by means other than the five physical senses, otherwise known as the "Sixth Sense," including clairvoyance, clairaudience, and clairsentience.

Exorcism: A ritual used to remove or banish entities thought to possess person or animal, or haunt a location. Often a member of a religious organization will perform the ritual.

Fetch: or "co-walker," One's double, seen by persons with clairvoyant ability at the time of a family member's death. Occasionally the fetch has been seen weeks or months before a person's death.

Full Apparition: When a spirit manifests as a full or nearly full body, either transparent or solid.

Gaussmeter: See EMF

GESP: General Extrasensory Perception. ESP in which it is unclear whether the results are due to telepathy, precognition, clairvoyance, or retrocognition.

Ghost: The apparition or spirit of a deceased person, which may or may not be visible.

Ghost Hunting: A controlled research project in which various methods and equipment are used to investigate reports of ghosts and hauntings.

Haunting: Recurring ghostly phenomena associated with spirits. Hauntings are usually associated with locations rather than persons.

Hellhound or Black Dog: A ghostly dog that appears just before death. Also associated with negative spirit hauntings.

Incubus: A demon in male form who lies upon sleeping women.

Kinetic Energy: Energy needed to force an object at rest into motion. Objects in motion have kinetic energy. (Also see Telekinesis)

Kirlian photography: a form of photogram made with a high voltage, named after Semyon Kirlian who accidentally discovered that if an object on a photographic plate is connected to a source of high voltage it will show the aura.

Ley Lines: Theoretical lines, possibly related to the magnetic fields of the earth, connecting ancient and modern sites around the world. Alfred Watkins first used the term in the 1920's after noticing that many structures could be connected by straight lines, and that some had relationships to star alignments. Intersections of these lines are said to have spiritual energy and certain structures are often found at these intersections. Some clairvoyants can see the ley lines, and they are often located by dowsing.

Levitation: To lift or raise an object in apparent defiance of gravity.

Matrix: A web-like structure, only visible to psychics, which connects everything in the universe and provides information to those who can tap into it. Not yet fully understood.

Manifestation: When an entity such as a ghost tries to make itself known to the living and creates a visible form, or partially visible form.

Materialization: The act of forming a shape in the air that is recognizable.

Medium: A psychic who regularly talks to the spirit world. Often someone who is clairaudient, clairsentient, and clairvoyant. Mediums may conduct séances.

Mist: Possibly related to an entity attempting to manifest itself, a visible mist or fog–like formation, usually indoors, that is unexplainable.

Motor Automatism: Spirit control over a person's body, as in automatic writing.

Dear Death Experience or NDE: An experience reported by people who have been clinically dead and revived, then report encounters with spirits, angels, dead relatives and sometimes a life review and out of the body experience. Some people who have had an NDE become intuitive, psychic, or more empathic. Some even have a complete personality change. Most no longer fear death.

Night Vision: Infrared (IR) radiation is electromagnetic radiation whose wavelength is longer than that of visible light. The name means "below red" (from the Latin *infra*, "below"), red being the color of visible light with the longest wavelength. Infrared radiation has wavelengths between about 750. Infrared is used in night vision equipment and is used when there is insufficient visible light to see normally.

The Ghost Hunter's Field Guide

Orb: An anomalous object, usually an independent light source that does not illuminate other objects and is believed to be spirits of the dead or other beings. Orbs typically range in size from the size of a pea to three feet in diameter and have been associated with haunting and portals. Orbs sometimes are visible to the naked eye, but appear more often on video or still photos. Orbs can change shapes, size, and can contain faces or geometric patterns. Orbs are still not fully understood by the paranormal community.

Ouija Board: A board used to communicate with spirits. A planchette is used by two people who lightly touch it to allow the spirit to spell out words or point to yes or no answers. Often the use of a Ouija board by inexperienced persons can lead to opening communication with a negative entity rather than the desired spirit.

Out-of-body Experience or OBE: A sensation or experience in which ones self or spirit travels to a different location than their physical body. OBE's are associated with involuntary astral projection.

Paranormal: Events that cannot be explained by conventional means and are out of the range of normal everyday occurrences or current scientific knowledge.

Parapsychology: The scientific study of paranormal phenomena coined by J.B Rhine.

Phantom or Ghost: Something that is seen, heard, or sensed, but has no physical reality. Also called a phantasm.

Poltergeist: Associated with physical activity such as thrown objects, breaking dishes, fire starting, stone throwing, lifting objects, etc. and may be related to a real "noisy" spirit or an adolescent female in the house who generates excess energy unconsciously. Literally means "Noisy Spirit."

Portal: In theory, an opening to another dimension or time.

Possession: When a person's body is apparently taken over by another personality or entity. Associated with mediumship and demonic possession.

Psychic: Someone who has one or more abilities to see, hear, or sense out of the normal range of most people- this ability is often called extra-sensory perception or ESP for short.

Psychical Research: The branch of science concerned with the study of Extrasensory perception and psychokinesis.

Psychokinesis (PK): or Telekinesis from the Greek "kinesis", meaning motion. The influence of the mind on physical items, i.e. moving or bending objects.

Psychometry: The ability to obtain knowledge by holding a physical object owned by a person.

Radio Voice Phenomenon or RVP: Receiving the voice of a deceased human being through a regular radio (usually AM).

Remote Viewer: Someone who projects their consciousness to another location, looks around, and describes or draws what they see at that location. Some remote viewers are very accurate, and some have the ability to look into the past or future when remote viewing.

Retrocognition: Paranormal knowledge of past events.

Séance: A gathering of people who attempt to receive messages from ghosts or spirits, or to listen to a spirit medium speak with or relay messages from spirits. Should be facilitated by an experienced medium.

Shadow person: (or entity) A term used to describe dark, usually human-like menacing forms. A phenomenon that is not completely understood.

Shape-Shifting: The ability to assume the form of another person, animal or other entity.

Simulcra: The seeing of faces, figures, and images in everyday objects such as walls, rocks, carpet, foliage, etc.

Sleep Paralysis: A state between sleep and awake, where a person is unable to move.

Speaking in Tongues: Unintelligible or unknown speech uttered in a trance state.

Specter: A ghostly apparition or phantom.

Spirit: The essence of a human being, animal, or other living thing. Spirits maintain their previous life personality (in my experience).

The Ghost Hunter's Field Guide

Spiritualism: The belief system that the dead are able to communicate with the living, through an intermediary or medium.

Spontaneous Human Combustion: Rare cases where a badly burned body is found with little or no damage to surrounding structures, suspected to originate inside the body of the victim.

Stigmata: The appearance of unexplained marks or open wounds on the body corresponding to the location to the crucifixion wounds of Christ in the feet, hands, or wrists. Usually only experienced by very devout Catholics.

Succubus: A demon in female form who lies with men while they are sleeping.

Subject: A person who is being studied or investigated.

Supernatural: Opposite of natural—phenomena having to do with divine or demonic intervention or experience.

Table-Tilting or Table-Tipping: Unexplained movement of a table, usually during a séance where a group of people join hands or touch fingers around the table.

Target: The objet or vent which a subject attempts to perceive, usually has to do with ESP testing.

Telekinesis: The ability to move or distort objects by using the mind to project energy. I.e. bending spoons using the mind.

Telepathy: Communication via extra-sensory-perception rather than the five senses. Awareness of another person's experience.

Often used in ghost hunting to communicate with deceased persons.

Third Eye: The area between the eyes on the forehead that is the location used as a means of communication by psychics or clairvoyants. This area will often buzz or tingle when the psychic is using it. Some psychics mentally "turn the third eye on" or activate it consciously, before sending their consciousness out to view anything.

Thought Form: An apparition of a being or object produced solely by the power of the human mind or collectively as a group.

Time Imprint: (also known as an Imprint or Residual Haunting) Similar to watching a movie, a time imprint is the energy left behind by activity, usually repeated over and over again in a specific location. There is no ghost or spirit, just the energy of the person or objects. A time imprint will not interact with people.

Trance: An altered state of consciousness, self-induced or induced by a hypnotist in order to access the subconscious mind and communicate with entities such as spirits, or guides.

Transpersonal Psychology: The study of practices and believes that suggest that the sense of self can extend beyond our physical reality.

Tree Spirit: Spirits who live inside of trees. May have been human in previous lifetimes and will often manifest their likeness in the bark or knots in the tree. Tree spirits can communicate telepathically with humans.

Tree Sprite: A Non-human entity or elemental who help trees grow, flower, leaf, grow limbs, and go dormant. Usually visible as tiny bright white/blue orbs which are in constant movement around trees. Tree sprites can communicate telepathically with humans, and may be visible to some psychics or with night vision equipment. There are usually a great number of tree sprites around trees.

Unidentified Flying Object (UFO): Unexplained objects in the sky often associated with alien visitation or visitation from people from the future. Also associated with Underwater Submerged Objects (USO).

Veridical dream: A dream that corresponds to events that are unknown to the dreamer, but later confirmed by facts and events.

Vortex: In theory—a portal or doorway to other dimensions, possibly linked to Ley Lines and electromagnetic fields of the earth. Often appears as a funnel or rope-like tube, possibly a wormhole in time-space.

White Noise: Use of a television turned to a channel with no programming, or a radio tuned to a frequency without programming in order to hear or see ghosts. White noise CD's are also available. It is thought that ghosts are able to communicate more easily while white noise is played. Fans can also produce white noise.

Worm Hole: A theoretical entity or topological feature allowed by Einstein's theory of general relativity in which space/time curvature connects two distant locations or times, allowing for a "shortcut" through space/time..

Bibliography

Barton, John, and John Muddiman, eds. "The Oxford Bible Commentary." New York: Oxford University Press, 2001.

Belanger, Jeff. "The World's Most Haunted Places." Fall River Press, 2004

Bord, Janet, "Fairies: Real Encounters With Little People, Mass Market Paperback

Brooks, Claire M. "A Cultivator's View of Reincarnation Cases in Western Medical Research." <u>Reincarnation Cases</u> 2003. August 2004 www.pureinsight.org/pi/articles/2002/9/2/213p.html.

Cannon, Timothy L. and Whitmore, Nancy F. "Ghosts & Legends of Frederick County"

Eason, Cassandra. "The Modern-day Druids." Platkus, 2003

Friedman, Stanton and Marden, Kathleen, "Science Was Wrong" New Page Books, 2010

Guiley, Rosemary Ellen. "The Encyclopedia of Ghost and Spirits." Visionary Living, Inc, 2007

Haining, Peter. "The Mammoth book of Haunted House Stories" 2005

Hollis, Heidi. *"The Secret War: The Heavens Speak of the Battle."* Author House, 2001. w*ww.shadows.ufo2u.com.*

Kirk, Robert, "The Secret Common-Wealth, edited with a commentary by Stewart Sanderson, D.S. Brewer, Suffolk, and Rowman and Littlefield, N.J., 1976

Knight, Sirona. "Fairy Magick." New Page books, 2003

Offutt, Jason. "Haunted Missouri: A Ghostly Guide to the Show-Me State's Most Spirited Spots." Truman University Press 2007

Offutt, Jason. "Darkness Walks: The Shadow People Among Us" Anomalist Books 2009

Riccio, Delores. "Haunted Houses U.S.A." 1989

Taylor, Troy. "Spirits of the Civil War." 1999

Van Praagh, James. "Ghost Among Us. Uncovering the Truth About the Other Side" Harper One, May 13, 2008.

Winkowski, Mary Ann, "When Ghosts Speak: Understanding the World of Earthbound spirits" Mass Market Paperback, Oct. 1, 2009

Websites:

Wikipedia: en.wikipedia.org/wiki/Paranormal.

Yahoo Dictionary: www.yahoo.com.

Paranormal news: www.paranormalnews.com.

Paranormal Dictionary: www.studiesoftheparanormal.com

The Mystica website.
themystica.com/mystica/articles/p/poltergeist.html.

Mystical Blaze: www.mysticalblaze.com

Frederic Gimino, the Free Psychic network,
www.freepsychicnetwork.com

Haunted America Tours, www.hauntedamericatours.com

From The Shadows: from-the-shadows.blogspot.com

The Faery-Faith Network: www.faeryfaith.org

Fairy Source: www.fairysource.com

Shadow People—the Psychic Detective: the-psychic-detective.com/shadow-People.htm

Demonology: www.djmcadam.com/demons.htm

The Certified Haunted House

Some hotel and restaurant owners want proof that their site is haunted in order to use this for promotional purposes. When we certify that a place as haunted we go through all of the procedures mentioned in this book and do our own investigation on site. We may return several times to the same place. If we find several anomalous things about a location that cannot be explained any other way, we may issue a Certified Haunted Location certificate or plaque. For more information please visit www.questig.com.

Sample:

Certified Haunted House

This house has been investigated by the
QUEST Investigation Group
paranormal research team.
We found this property to be
haunted by one or more spirits.
Enter at your own risk.

Signature: _____
Margie Kay
Director
QUEST Investigation Group
Date: _____

Index

1, 252
1859 Jackson County Jail, 211
Agate, 114, 115
Akashic record, 40
Alcatraz, 211
alcohol, 54
aliens, 12, 26, 28, 29, 34, 37, 41, 132
Aliens, 3, 26, 41, 123
Amber, 115
Amulet, 229
angels, 12, 37, 63, 235
Anomalous, 229
Antietam, 206
Apparition, 229, 231, 233
apparitions, 14, 28, 37, 60, 82, 131, 138, 146, 159, 197, 199, 201, 206, 207, 208, 209, 217, 218
Apparitions, 210, 211
Aquamarine, 115
Asport, 229
astral body, 13, 23, 229
Astral Body, 229
Astral Plane, 229
Astral Projection, 229
Astral Travel, 23
Aura, 229
Automatic Writing, 230
Automatism, 230, 235
Autoscopy, 230
Ax Murder House, 196
Baby powder, 69
Bachelors Grove, 199
Ball Lightning, 3, 38, 230
Banshee, 230
Battlefields, 206
Bell Witch, 212, 213
black, 9, 17, 31, 32, 42, 43, 45, 52, 60, 64, 106, 110, 114, 122, 131, 134, 138, 140, 141, 144, 152, 153, 161, 162, 175, 176, 183, 216, 217
Blair Witch', 219
Blogtalkradio, 221
Blue chalcedony, 114, 115
camera, 67, 69, 71, 82, 83, 84, 104, 106, 127, 129, 130, 138, 147, 154, 156, 159, 160, 195, 218, 231
Cemeteries, 199
Channeling, 230
Chickamouga, and Chattanooga, 207
Children, 16, 99, 190
Chillingham Castle, 215
chimneys, 101, 152, 163, 164, 167, 168, 232
Clairaudience, 62
Clairaudient, 230
Clairsentience, 59
Clairsentient, 230
Clairvoyance, 60
Clairvoyant, 231
Coast to Coast AM, 220
Cold Harbor Battlefield, 208
Cold spot, 231
Coleman Theatre, 205
consciousness, 26, 39, 50, 51, 54, 61, 229, 237, 240
Courthouse Exchange, 204
Crystals, 6, 106, 111, 113
David Icke's, 36
Dear Death Experience
  NDE, 235
death, 13, 20, 21, 23, 24, 25, 26, 29, 47, 61, 62, 186, 194, 196, 198, 203, 213, 214, 217, 230, 231, 232, 233, 234, 235
Déjà vu, 22, 63
Deja' vu, 231
Demons, 3, 35
devil, 35, 231
Digital Camera, 67, 231
Digital Cameras, 3, 67, 226
Digital Thermometer, 3, 66
Digital Voice Recorder, 68
dimension, 12, 13, 14, 28, 43, 50, 121, 123, 153, 237
Direct Voice Phenomenon, 231
  DVP, 231
divining, 74
Doppelganger, 231
dowsing, 3, 54, 58, 64, 69, 74, 76, 78,

79, 110, 157, 234
Dowsing, 3, 54, 69, 74, 76, 113, 232
Dowsing Rods, 3, 69, 76
Dowsing,, 74
Dracula's Castle, 213
Draft, 168, 232
dream, 27, 63, 241
Earthbound, 232, 244
Eastern State Penitentiary, 212
Ectoplasm, 232
Edinburgh, 214
electro-magnetic fields, 99, 100, 232
Electronic Voice Phenomenon EVP, 232
Elementals, 232
elves, 33, 232
EMF detector, 106
EMF Detector, 3, 67, 232
energy, 8, 12, 25, 31, 35, 37, 38, 40, 42, 44, 46, 55, 67, 74, 76, 79, 85, 107, 110, 111, 112, 114, 115, 120, 132, 143, 144, 147, 157, 168, 175, 178, 229, 234, 237, 239, 240
energy field, 12, 114
energy fields, 8, 55
Entity, 232
evil, 35, 36, 45, 46, 115, 231
Exorcism, 233
Extra Sensory Perception, 8, 233
Faery, 34, 245
fairies, 12, 33, 34, 37, 102, 232
Fairies, 3, 33, 243
fairy, 33, 147
Fetch, 233
fireplaces, 163, 165, 168
Fog and Apparitions, 3, 37
Forts, 206
General Washington's, 208
George Noory, 220
GESP, 233
Gettysburg, 206
Ghost, 1, 2, 3, 6, 10, 65, 66, 106, 108, 109, 116, 183, 190, 223, 233, 236, 243, 244, 252
ghost hunting, 10, 11, 19, 28, 29, 36, 41, 44, 53, 59, 66, 68, 70, 74, 76, 77, 82, 84, 87, 91, 93, 100, 103,

106, 110, 111, 117, 156, 160, 225, 231, 240
Ghost hunting, 10
Ghost Trains, 183
ghosts, 8, 9, 10, 12, 14, 19, 26, 28, 29, 40, 41, 43, 47, 50, 55, 57, 63, 64, 66, 67, 68, 69, 70, 76, 90, 92, 94, 95, 96, 99, 100, 102, 107, 108, 117, 118, 120, 131, 132, 136, 146, 148, 150, 153, 161, 164, 167, 168, 181, 189, 191, 193, 196, 197, 200, 201, 202, 203, 204, 205, 207, 208, 209, 211, 212, 214, 217, 218, 219, 220, 229, 231, 232, 233, 238, 241
Ghosts, 3, 11, 26, 49, 59, 81, 89, 92, 107, 117, 123, 133, 140, 148, 163, 185, 209, 215, 216, 219, 243, 244, 252
Glore Psychiatric Museum, 200
gnomes, 33, 34, 232
Hallucinations, 101
haunted, 28, 57, 65, 90, 91, 94, 100, 113, 117, 131, 142, 152, 158, 166, 173, 176, 182, 189, 197, 198, 200, 201, 202, 205, 206, 207, 209, 211, 214, 216, 217, 218, 219, 223, 246, 252
Haunted, 6, 117, 131, 155, 161, 163, 173, 195, 197, 198, 204, 212, 223, 243, 244, 245, 246, 252
haunting, 40, 44, 47, 52, 59, 66, 69, 97, 100, 102, 130, 153, 160, 161, 198, 202, 206, 213, 236
Haunting, 92, 154, 233, 240
Hellhound
 Black dog, 234
Hypnosis, 57, 61, 226
Independence, 2, 83, 84, 90, 117, 131, 133, 145, 148, 151, 158, 161, 177, 179, 183, 184, 190, 191, 196, 198, 199, 204, 210, 211, 251, 252
intuitive, 10, 29, 41, 59, 63, 95, 235
Ireland, 24, 33, 34
Jamaica, 194
Jekyll Island, 204
Kinetic Energy, 234
Kirlian photography, 234

Labradorite, 115
Lady in Red, 158, 159
Landers Theater, 205
Laser Thermometer, 3, 66, 104
Laularie House, 213
Lecher, 3, 31
Lemp Mansion, 201
Levitation, 234
Ley Lines, 234, 241
light photons, 13, 22, 25, 37, 47
Lincoln Theater, 205
Lindsey Porter, 190, 191, 192, 193
Little Bighorn, 207
Lizzie Bordon, 201
Mammoth, 218, 243
Manifestation, 234
Marie Laveau, 200
Materialization, 235
Matrix, 40, 234
Meditation, 3, 51, 63, 225
medium, 33, 98, 157, 230, 232, 238, 239
Medium, 235
Michio Kaku, 13
Mist, 94, 235
Myrtles Plantation, 200
negative, 33, 35, 36, 42, 44, 45, 47, 48, 52, 53, 55, 79, 107, 110, 111, 113, 114, 115, 120, 132, 143, 178, 232, 234, 236
Night Vision, 3, 68, 235
Night Vision Monocular, 68
Nightwatch, 221
Noland Road Lady in Grey., 199
Obsidian, 114, 115
Orb, 94, 236
orbs, 12, 22, 34, 36, 37, 47, 60, 67, 83, 138, 147, 163, 164, 168, 172, 181, 187, 189, 207, 209, 241
Orbs, 3, 36, 82, 236
Ordsall Hall-, 198
Ouija Board, 236
Out-of-body Experience, 236
paranormal, 8, 14, 28, 29, 41, 43, 64, 69, 93, 94, 96, 118, 122, 130, 133, 135, 143, 144, 153, 155, 157, 158, 160, 161, 163, 165, 167, 172, 195, 199, 202, 203, 211, 214, 220, 221, 222, 223, 232, 236, 251
Paranormal, 6, 41, 103, 201, 220, 221, 222, 223, 228, 236, 238, 245
Parapsychology, 236
Park, 83, 84, 145, 147, 199, 202, 206, 207, 217, 218
pendulum, 58, 69, 74, 75, 76, 97, 110, 113, 186, 191, 232
Pendulums, 3, 69
Plasma, 3, 38
Plymouth, 208, 217
poltergeist, 32, 33, 38, 111, 131, 203, 229, 245
Poltergeist, 3, 32, 236
poltergeists, 12
Poltergeists, 32
Portal, 121, 237
possession, 35, 36, 99, 149, 231, 237
Possession, 99, 237
Psychic, 63, 102, 115, 237, 245
Psychical Research, 237
Psychics, 3, 14, 69
Psychokinesis, 237
Psychometry, 237
Radio, 6, 220, 221, 222, 237
Remote Viewer, 237
Reptilian, 35
Riverstone, 115
rods, 12, 55, 69, 74, 76, 77, 157, 232
Roger Marsh, 221
Salem, 217
Sam Porter, 190
San Antonio, 207, 218
Séance, 238
seeing, 7, 8, 31, 42, 44, 55, 57, 59, 64, 101, 102, 142, 154, 174, 207, 213, 214, 230, 238
Shadow People, 41, 144, 244, 245
Shadow person, 238
Shape-Shifting, 238
Sixth Sense, 59, 233
Sleep Paralysis, 238
smoke., 54, 187
soul, 22, 23, 25, 26, 42, 127
Speaking in Tongues, 238
Specter, 238

Spirit, 3, 39, 86, 235, 237, 238, 240
spirit body, 22, 23, 47
Spirit Fog, 3, 39, 86
Spirits, 3, 13, 20, 26, 27, 39, 40, 50, 73, 109, 116, 142, 198, 238, 240, 243, 244
Spiritualism, 239
Spontaneous Human Combustion, 239
Stigmata, 239
Subject, 239
Succubus, 239
sugar, 54
Supernatural, 239
Syracuse Landmark Theater, 206
Table-Tilting, 239
Target, 239
Telekinesis, 234, 237, 239
telepathically, 8, 19, 21, 39, 40, 130, 186, 191, 192, 240, 241
telepathy, 8, 28, 55, 233
Telepathy, 239
The 1886 Crescent Hotel, 203
The Alamo, 207, 218
The Capital Building, 216
The Catacombs, 213
The Coliseum, 214
The Deane House, 197
The Hotel Savoy, 202
The Hyatt–, 202
The Music Hall, 204
The New Castle, 214
The Queen Mary, 215
The Sagamore, 203
The Stanley Hotel, 202
The Tower of London, 212
The Truman Home, 196
The Vaile Mansion, 198
The Whaley House, 197
The White House, 216

Third Eye, 240
Thought Form, 240
Thurnham Hall, 180
Time Imprint, 3, 14, 31, 160, 240
Tina Porter, 190, 193
Tombstone, 217
Toumaline, 115
trance, 21, 23, 24, 25, 26, 33, 35, 40, 53, 61, 98, 108, 130, 131, 134, 135, 146, 149, 151, 154, 156, 157, 190, 192, 193, 229, 238
Tree Sprite, 241
Tree Sprites, 3, 39
Tuatha De Dannan', 34
TV, 6, 43, 127, 167, 181, 198, 204, 220, 223
UFO, 8, 28, 35, 37, 41, 68, 75, 94, 153, 203, 221, 241, 252
Underground Vaults, 214
Unidentified Flying Object, 241
Union Station, 215
UV Light, 3, 69
Valley Forge, 208
vegetarian diet, 50, 54
vibratory rate, 12, 27, 50, 54
Victorian, 90, 175, 185, 186, 198, 201
video, 37, 66, 67, 71, 82, 97, 103, 147, 156, 187, 220, 223, 225, 232, 236
visible light spectrum, 14
Vortex, 39, 241
water witching, 74
Waverly Hills Sanatorium, 200
White light, 110
White Noise, 3, 70, 104, 222, 241
White Witch of Rose Hall, 194
Winchester Mystery House, 196
Wind Meter, 3, 69
Woodlawn Cemetery, 199
Worm Hole, 241
Zener Cards, 56

About the Author

Margie Kay is a native of the Kansas City area and lives in Independence, Missouri with her husband, Gene, where they operate a contracting business. Margie is a nationally known speaker, has written numerous articles for magazines and newspapers, and is the author of over a dozen books on various topics. She was host of QUEST radio show on KCXL for five years, and has been a guest on several national radio and T.V. programs.

Kay's interest in the paranormal began at a very early age. She showed psychic abilities before the age of five, and began to see spirits at the age of 11. Kay's natural abilities to see through objects and people, predict events, and do remote real-time or viewing the past has astounded many. She has the special gift of medical diagnosis and viewing the interior of bodies to see where problem areas are. Kay often does on the spot readings at conferences so the entire audience can see the results.

Kay's abilities have led to solving many missing person cases and homicides. Law enforcement and private investigators from all over the world call on her to help with difficult and unsolved cases. The QUEST Investigation Group, which includes two of Kay's psychic daughters and other professionals, work together to help solve crimes and do haunted location investigations and certifications nationwide.

Margie is the Assistant State Director for Missouri MUFON, and director of the annual **Mysteries of the Universe Conference** in Kansas City, Missouri where internationally known researchers share their experiences and research. She is available for speaking engagements. Visit www.margiekay.com for more information.

Books and Films by 7 Planet Productions

Haunted Independence by Margie Kay 2009
The Ghost Hunter's Field Guide by Margie Kay 2010
The UFO Hunter's Field Guide by Margie Kay 2010
High Strangeness in Butler, Missouri: a film by Margie Kay 2011
Welcome to Earth book and documentary film by Margie Kay (coming soon)
After-Affects of UFO Encounters by Margie Kay (coming soon)
Color Therapy Wall Chart by Margie Kay 1999

Visit www.margiekay.com

Books by Maria Christine
Chillingly True Ghost Stories 2007
Parallel: New Beginnings and Old Ghosts (fiction) 2 010
The Seventh Dimension (fiction) 2011

Visit www.mariachristineonline.com